Tigga Mac's CAKE HACKS

Tigga Mac began her cake decorating journey with her best mate **Katie** in their own tiny kitchen over seven years ago. Katie could bake. Tigga could decorate. Combining these two ingredients allowed them to turn their dream of starting their own business into a reality.

Since then, Tigga has become a viral phenomenon, known for her incredible cake decorating skills, iconic voiceovers and signature 'Okie dokie' catchphrase. Her social media audience has grown into a following of over 4 million people across multiple platforms, allowing Tigga and Katie to help make cake decorating and custom-themed cakes accessible to everyone.

EBURY PRESS

Tegan MacCormack & Katie Scoble

Tigga Mac's CAKE HACKS

Unbelievably fun and easy children's birthday cakes

Step-by-step cake creations that won't break the bank

1

Ebury Press, an imprint of Ebury Publishing
20 Vauxhall Bridge Road
London SW1V 2SA

Ebury Press is part of the Penguin Random House group of companies
whose addresses can be found at global.penguinrandomhouse.com

First published in Australia by Penguin Books in 2024
This edition published by Ebury Press in 2024

www.penguin.co.uk

Cover and internal photography by Brent Parker Jones
Food styling by Meryl Batlle
Cover and internal design by Adam Laszczuk © Penguin Random House Australia Pty Ltd
Internal images by AspctStyle/Shutterstock, Virinaflora/Shutterstock, ardeastudio/Shutterstock,
Alex Gorka/Shutterstock, samui/Shutterstock
Typeset by Post Pre-press, Australia
Index by Puddingburn Publishing, Australia

Printed and bound in Germany by MOHN Media

A CIP catalogue record for this book is available from the British Library

ISBN 978 1 529 92967 6

The authorised representative in the EEA is Penguin Random House Ireland, Morrison Chambers, 32
Nassau Street, Dublin D02 YH68.

Penguin Random House is committed to a sustainable future for our business, our readers and our
planet. This book is made from Forest Stewardship Council® certified paper.

This book is dedicated to you! The reader.

It belongs to anyone who wants to give cake decorating a go! Cakes are made to be destroyed and enjoyed but the memory of celebrating life's big moments with these cakes will last forever.

Happy caking!

Contents

WHIMSICAL & WONDERFUL   23

FARMYARD FRIENDS   63

TRACKS, WHEELS & AUTOMOBILES 93

SLIMY SCALES, TEETH & TAILS 121

CREEPY, KOOKY & ALL THINGS SPOOKY 157

TRUE AUSSIE DELIGHTS 179

A Message to the Reader

Okie dokie and g'day!

Welcome to the world of *Tigga Mac's Cake Hacks!* This book has been a long-time dream, and it feels quite surreal it is now finally here!! Both Katie and I appreciate you purchasing this book and letting us play a small part in your life's most precious celebrations!

I have been creating custom-made cakes for over 12 years, but I started with no training and no experience. Just a love for design and a desire to create!

Being completely self-taught, Katie and I believe it is so important that the world of cake decorating should remain open to everyone, regardless of their ability. Everyone deserves to have a cake on their birthday. And by following the steps in this book, you can create a cake that will bring a smile to anyone's face!

The world of culinary art and the science of baking can feel so intimidating and unachievable, but we are here to bust that myth and show you that YOU CAN hack your way to birthday cake success!

Tigga Mac's Cake Hacks is not just a cake decorating guide, it's an experience. We want to get people back into the kitchen. Help you slow down and be present. Encourage you to be willing to get a little messy! This is your chance to take a break from the daily grind and relieve the mental load with a little fun and creativity. To not only bake FOR your children but WITH your children.

If you have never decorated or baked a cake before, this book is the perfect starting point for you. For those of you who do have experience in cake decorating, we hope this book provides you with even more knowledge and inspiration to help you along the way!

All our hacks have varying degrees of difficulty. Each chapter is ordered from the simplest to the most challenging! This way, you can start with the most basic hacks and progressively build your confidence. We are completely certain that you will surprise yourself with how much you can actually achieve in your own kitchen!

We encourage everyone who gives these hacks a go to use our creations as a guide. Yes, we are here to provide the spark, but your imagination is lighting the fire! Pick your favourite colours, your favourite flavours. If you want to add crazy eyebrows or a tail, GO FOR IT!

In terms of nailing the technical aspects of decorating, rest assured that you can choose any cake in this book, and Katie and I will be here to hold your hand from start to finish. Read our hacks and let the photos guide you! And for the more difficult hacks in this book, you can scan the QR codes provided and decorate alongside ME by watching our video tutorials!

This book will provide everything you need to create the centrepiece of any celebration! Yes, they are perfect for birthdays, but you can turn any day into a celebration. Sometimes it's just about bringing a little extra sweetness into the lives of those you love.

It doesn't matter if you're not a baker, and it doesn't matter if you use a packet mix or a store-bought cake then do the decorating yourself. You can still make it your own! You can achieve that sense of pride that comes from creating something with your own two hands. It's not about perfection. In fact, it's about letting go of perfectionism and simply giving it a red-hot go!

Throwing children's parties and baking cakes doesn't need to be a competition. Some of my best childhood memories come from the simple process of creating. At the end of the day, the person receiving this cake will adore it because it was made by you. That will always be enough.

Cakes are made to be destroyed and enjoyed! Memories are forever.

Have fun making memories!

Tigga X

Our Story

On an ordinary Monday morning, a small blonde-haired, blue-eyed girl named Tigga sat alone on a school bench. At eight years old, she had just moved to a new town, started a new school and knew nobody. I saw Tigga sitting alone and shyly introduced myself, neither of us having any clue that on this ordinary Monday morning, a lifelong friendship would begin, a friendship that would forever alter both of our lives.

As our friendship thrived over the years, Tigga took her talent in design and began her career as a cake decorator. Despite having no formal training, her skills advanced through hours of practice and repetition. She began to push the boundaries and create incredible cake designs.

From the beginning, I would watch on in awe of my friend's talents. Taking on a cheerleading role, I encouraged Tigga to recognise her extraordinary skills and dream bigger! I'd always had a passion for all things SUGAR. From a young age I loved baking cakes and desserts and quickly developed an unrivalled sweet tooth!

Over coffee we often discussed a shared vision of owning our own business together. The plan was to convert a small spare room in my home into a cake kitchen and combine my passion for baking and Tigga's talent for decorating.

That was all we had – talent, passion and an empty spare room. It turns out, that's all we needed.

Tigga began filming her cake designs on her phone and posting them across social media. She combined her cakes with relatable and down-to-earth voiceovers. These now iconic voiceovers, starting with the catchphrase 'Okie dokie!', described the decorating process in a way that became accessible for everyone.

Through social media we invited the world into our tiny kitchen. Suddenly Tigga's cakes were being seen by millions. The world we created online became a landscape of warmth and joy. A sugar-filled source of escapism.

It's hard to believe where this journey has taken us. We began just wanting to create cakes for our local community. Once the doors were open to the rest of the world the opportunities we were given were mind-boggling.

The hilarity of trying to hide hyper-realistic cakes on supermarket shelves, fooling our audience as well as the unsuspecting shoppers!

The nerves of appearing on live TV and radio interviews.

The exhaustion and exhilaration of creating seven cakes in seven days for Disney!

The awe and stress of leaving our little kitchen to take a replica vacuum cake on a 4-hour plane journey all the way to Central Australia.

The thrill of travelling and teaching workshops and hearing in person how our videos have inspired so many kids to start baking and so many adults to start their own businesses.

It's honestly been incredibly rewarding and a privilege to wake up every day and not know exactly what is coming – but to no longer feel that any of it is out of reach.

Even this book. We could have never foreseen we would be able to do this. To imagine people all across the globe recreating our designs completely blows our minds!

Throughout the entire crazy journey of building a business, our friendship has remained the number-one priority. When decorating, Tigga's joyful voiceovers are authentic because behind every creation are two best mates coming up with crazy ideas and bringing them to life! Even with the mistakes along the way (and there have been many!) the main soundtrack to our journey has been laughter.

We have ridden the sugar highs and lows together. The key ingredient to the Tigga Mac brand's success will always be friendship. Everything else is just icing on the cake!

Katie x

Don't Skip This Page!

I know, right?! Who even reads all the 'important info' at the beginning of a recipe? Well, I figured it was my duty as a cake decorator of more than 12 years to share all the helpful hints and knowledge I have learned along the way. I made the mistakes and worked out the solutions, so you don't have to!

Aussie, Aussie, Aussie!

Yes, this is an Australian book and we are Australian, but rest assured that the designs are for absolutely everybody worldwide!

We have tried to make the book as accessible as possible. We have provided a metric to imperial kitchen conversion chart at the back of the book (see page 209) to make use of if needed. Also, some ingredients might not be available where you are, but you can always find equivalents from locations near you or alter the design slightly to make it your own! Simply use the photos as a guide for what is required in each hack!

Also, you'll find lots of Aussie phrases and words, but don't worry, the instructions are clear and the photos will provide a visual guide to help you find what you need!

Work your way up!

Tigga Mac's Cake Hacks is made up of six FUN-FILLED chapters. All of our hacks are given a level of difficulty – EASY PEASY, MEDIUM or IT'S A CHALLENGE! – perfect for any degree of skill, from beginners to the more advanced decorators. We haven't done this to scare you out of doing the more challenging cakes. We just felt it was a great way to give you as much information as possible going into each hack.

Plan ahead

There are many steps involved in decorating a cake, so planning ahead will help make the whole process much more seamless. For example, baking your cake in advance will give you one less thing to do in the lead-up to decorating your cake. You could make it the week before and freeze it, remove your cake the night before and defrost it in the fridge ready for decorating the next day, or bake the day before and simply refrigerate overnight.

Another thing you can do to plan ahead is to read over the cake hack in full beforehand, as this ensures you will have everything you need in terms of equipment and ingredients. Your buttercream can also be made in advance. Just store airtight in the fridge.

Don't hesitate, REFRIGERATE!

When it comes to cake decorating, the fridge is your friend! I will use a fridge throughout the entire cake decorating process, from shaping and assembly to covering a cake in buttercream. Even if you are using a store-bought cake, we recommend refrigerating before decorating! The reason for this is because a cold cake is much more cooperative. When cold, all the oils and moisture in the cake become firm, which makes carving and shaping so much easier.

It's also really important to chill your cake in between steps while decorating. The fridge will set your buttercream and make everything much sturdier. I know sometimes people can be impatient and might just want to move on to the next step, but chilling your cake will make that next step much easier, saving you time in the end. Trust me, it's worth it! Setting a timer can help you keep track of how long your cake has been in the fridge, so you don't rush it.

I can't say it enough: WHEN IN DOUBT, CHILL OUT! Just assembled your cake? REFRIGERATE! Just covered your cake in a crumb coat? REFRIGERATE! Just finished your cake? *REFRIGERATE!*

Crumb coat

I swear by the crumb coat! A crumb coat is the first coat of buttercream that catches all the crumbs from your cake. This first layer is then chilled until firm before the second (and final) coat of buttercream goes on.

I recommend doing a crumb coat because it will help you achieve a cleaner and neater result. Don't stress if you can see some cake through this first layer, as you will be doing a second coat anyway! We recommend using the same colour for your crumb coat as you will be using for the top coat, as it makes for a cleaner result.

Lastly, when applying your crumb coat, aim for a smooth finish, as this will help you achieve a smoother result overall, once you have added your top coat.

Let's get level

When you bake a cake, there is usually a dome in the centre where the cake has risen during the baking process. Before you start decorating, you will need to remove this dome by slicing it off to create a nice level cake. You want your cake to be as flat and level as possible before you begin the first step of your cake hack!

Clean as you go

To set yourself up for success, try to keep your cake decorating space as clean and clear as possible. There's nothing worse than picking up your palette knife only to realise there are cake crumbs all over it! I find it easiest to clean as I go, wiping the bench after each step and putting away any equipment I won't be needing anymore. A clean workspace will help create a stress-free environment and give you less clean-up at the end too!

Applying buttercream

With some of the cake hacks, I will advise you to apply your buttercream with a piping bag. This is because these cake shapes are a bit tricky and using a piping bag will give you so much more control over your buttercream application. You can ensure you have an even coverage and at the same time you won't disturb or ruin the shape of your cake. It also prevents cake crumbs from getting into your bowl of buttercream, which can occur when going back and forth with a palette knife.

Gel colours

For all our hacks you will see we use a gel-based food colouring. This is different from the liquid food dye you might be more familiar with. The reason we use gel colouring is because it is far more concentrated, which means you will use less colouring overall. Using a thicker gel rather than a liquid also means it won't alter the consistency and structure of your buttercream! Another great option is oil-based colours.

The lowdown on sweets

So many of our hacks contain Smarties or M&M's. These are a super simple and effective addition to our designs. However, they do not like being in the fridge. The moisture will make the colours bleed and fade. So, if you do make your cake the day before, I would recommend adding them onto the cake the day of the party.

Equipment

As a cake decorator, I have amassed a large amount of decorating equipment over the years. Some tools I use every day, others are a bit more niche. Here you will find my most used and favourite cake tools. The must-haves. The pieces of equipment that will make your job a whole lot easier. I have provided more common household substitutes where possible, but I do suggest adding these items to your cake decorating equipment must-haves!

Turntable

This would be my most loved and most used cake decorating tool. The humble turntable can turn a difficult task into a piece of cake (pun intended!). With the flick of a wrist, it gives you a full 360-degree view of your cake masterpiece and makes decorating SO. MUCH. EASIER.

Personally, I use an aluminium turntable as I prefer the heavy base and it spins easily and smoothly. But even a simple plastic turntable is a great place to start. Keep in mind, some turntables require a grip pad on top to keep your cake from slipping. You can use a non-slip mat found at your local grocery store and cut to size.

Rubber spatula

A rubber spatula is very handy when making your buttercream. Use it to scrape down your bowl, divide your buttercream and also to mix colours.

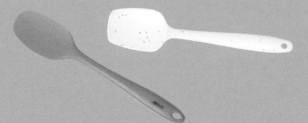

Palette knife

Palette knives are used to smooth buttercream over your cake. Yes, you could use a butter knife instead, but you will be at a disadvantage. Butter knives are skinnier than palette knives and they also have a slightly serrated edge on one side. This can make spreading your buttercream much harder and your end result won't be as neat.

Palette knives come in a few different sizes and shapes. My most used are the large straight palette knife and the small offset spatula. If you have both of these in your cake supplies, you're golden!

Stand mixer

I don't know where I would be without my trusty stand mixer. Our buttercream recipe does require a fair bit of mixing and using a stand mixer if possible is definitely the way to go. If you don't have a stand mixer, a hand-held electric beater is a good substitute, but keep in mind there will be lots of standing around holding that mixer, especially as our buttercream requires a stiff peak meringue.

Cake scraper

I use my cake scrapers A LOT. They come in lots of different lengths and are usually made from aluminium or plastic. You use a cake scraper to achieve a smooth result on the sides of your cake. My most used is a 18cm aluminium scraper. I find it's a great length for smaller cakes and is very useful for achieving sharp edges. It's definitely worth having in your cake supplies.

Large serrated knife

I use a long, serrated cake knife to cut and slice my cakes. A long bread knife could do the trick but if you can get your hands on a proper cake knife, you won't regret it! A cake knife is usually a bit longer than a bread knife, which comes in handy when slicing a cake horizontally.

Piping bag

I use piping bags a lot when decorating cakes. You can get them in both disposable and reusable options. I have found the disposable ones to be the most useful, as you can use them without adding a piping tip by cutting the end to the size required. You can get disposable piping bags that are biodegradable as well, which I highly recommend! I mostly use 30cm piping bags.

Piping tip

There are a LOT of different piping tips out there, many of which you will probably never use. For the cake hacks in this book, you will only need:

1. a star tip nozzle
2. a grass tip nozzle. You could substitute this one with a star tip if need be, but a grass tip nozzle does come in handy when wanting to create grass or hair
3. a round nozzle.

Cake board

When decorating a cake, having a nice flat board for your cake to sit on is a must! I would avoid using a plate or platter mostly because they are rarely completely flat. A round or square wooden chopping board could be a good alternative. Cake boards can usually be purchased from your local grocery store, cake supply store or online.

Cake tins

Cake tins can come in many different sizes and be made from different materials. A low cake tin won't work for Tigga Mac cake hacks as you will need a nice high cake to achieve the right look. The cake tins will need to be at least 7cm in height! Both of the cake recipes in this book (chocolate mud and vanilla velvet) have a runny batter and long cooking times, so we do not recommend a springform pan. We have found the recipes work best in a high-quality tin made from thick aluminium. Lower-quality tins may affect cooking times.

The *Tigga Mac* Philosophy

Cakes are for everyone!

You'll notice the cakes in this book are not categorised by age or gender. The Tigga Mac philosophy is that there is no such thing as 'cakes for boys' or 'cakes for girls'! Our cake hacks are designed by what sparks joy and ignites creativity for ANYONE!

Yes, you can!

'I'M JUST NOT A BAKER' 'I'VE NEVER BAKED ANYTHING IN MY LIFE'

These are the statements we hear ALL the time. Don't let these be the roadblocks that stop you from giving cake decorating a go. Yes, it's a cliché to say it's the thought that counts, but honestly, the fact that you have poured your time and effort into creating something for someone you love will bring more joy than any store-bought cake can!

I'm all about the exclamation mark!!!!!!!

You will notice this book is full of exclamation marks! That's because I'm all about keeping cake decorating fun and exciting! I'm loud and enthusiastic and every time you see an exclamation mark, I hope you hear my voice in your head, cheering you on!!

Cake is a treat. Treat ya-self!

We haven't provided any sugar-free alternatives in this book. Katie and I are all about the sugar rush! We are not nutritionists; we are here to provide joy-filled cake designs! Keep in mind, these cakes are for parties and occasions to indulge in occasionally. BUT we totally encourage everyone to explore any dietary requirement recipes and still use our designs to create beautiful cakes.

Do not compare!

Please remember I have been decorating for over 12 years and have decorated literally thousands of cakes! Your finished cake may look completely different to the photos in this book. If so, AWESOME!! That means you have created something unique, full of charm and personality.

You do you!

Don't expect to pick everything up first go. Cake decorating takes time and practice, so be patient with yourself. Being able to look back and see the progress you have made is so rewarding!

Have fun!!

Yes, it's easier said than done. But these hacks are about bringing a little joy into life! At the end of the day, it's just cake! Have fun with it!

Types of Cake

For each of our cake hacks, we are incredibly flexible about the types of cake or flavour you choose. We realise that people can be time poor or would simply prefer to use a store-bought cake or a packet cake mix! This is ABSOLUTELY fine!! *Tigga Mac's Cake Hacks* is a judgement-free zone!

Our simple aim is to set you up for success and to create the most enjoyable and hassle-free decorating experience possible.

Keep in mind: different types of cakes have very different consistencies and levels of stability. For example, your nana's classic Victorian sponge recipe (whilst being delicious!) will not carve well, which can make the assembly of your cake very difficult!

For most of our cake hacks we would recommend using a mud cake recipe. Not only are these deliciously moist, but they are also easy to handle, carve and shape, making them the perfect base for our hacks!

In *Tigga Mac's Cake Hacks*, we provide both a chocolate mud and a vanilla velvet recipe, along with our buttercream and ganache recipes, which pair perfectly!

Chocolate mud cakes are an ideal option because you can bake them in advance. The flavour will develop and improve over time and it relieves you of the burden and stress of baking when it comes to the day of decorating. Our vanilla velvet recipe is a lighter alternative option! This cake is still dense enough to carve and stack, but it has a more velvety crumb and a lighter texture.

Remember, this isn't about being the best baker in the world. It's about giving it a go and most of all having fun!

Happy baking!

Tigga's CHOCOLATE MUD CAKE

This delicious chocolate mud cake cooks for a long time at a low temperature, which locks in all the moisture. It has a long shelf life and also freezes well, so can be made in advance and thawed before use.

We always bake our cakes at least a day prior to decorating and refrigerate them overnight wrapped in cling film. This ensures the cake is cold before decorating, making it easier to carve and handle. It's the perfect cake for any Tigga Mac cake hack!

THIS RECIPE WILL YIELD EITHER:

1 × 20CM ROUND OR SQUARE CAKE

OR 2 × 15CM ROUND CAKES

The cake tin needs to be at least 7cm high. Many cake tins are only 3–4cm high but this recipe and the hacks won't work in a low tin.

PREP TIME – 30 minutes

COOK TIME – 1 hour 30 minutes

You Will Need

2 tablespoons canola oil

375g caster sugar

250g self-raising flour

25g cocoa

¾ teaspoon baking powder

225g unsalted butter

140g dark chocolate

300ml boiling water

1 teaspoon instant coffee granules
(de-caf, if you like)

2 large eggs

Scan for video tutorial!

1. Preheat the oven to 180°C (160°C fan-forced). Using cooking spray, grease your chosen cake tin (depending on the hack you are creating) and line the base and sides with baking paper.

2. In a mixing bowl combine the canola oil and caster sugar. Set aside.

3. In another bowl combine the flour, cocoa and baking powder. Set aside.

4. Melt the butter in a saucepan over low heat and then add the dark chocolate, then stir until melted and combined. Remove from the heat and set aside.

5. Carefully measure the boiling water in a heatproof jug, then add the coffee and stir. Add to the mixing bowl containing the oil and sugar. Using a whisk, mix until the sugar has dissolved.

6. Add the dry ingredients to the mixing bowl and whisk until combined. Scrape the sides of the bowl and then mix again for 1 minute.

7. Add the eggs and mix until combined.

8. Add the melted butter/chocolate mixture and give it one last mix to combine. The mixture should be smooth and easy to pour.

9. Pour the cake batter into the lined tin.

10. Cover the tin with foil before placing it in the preheated oven. The baking time will vary depending on the size of the cake or cakes you are making and your oven. In our oven, a 20cm chocolate mud cake takes 1 hour 20 minutes. We suggest setting the timer for 1 hour, then testing the centre of the cake with a skewer. If the skewer does not come out clean, this means your cake is not fully baked. Keep checking at regular intervals until the skewer comes out clean.

11. Once the cake has been removed from the oven, wait 15 minutes before turning it out onto a cooling rack. Wrap the cake in cling film while still warm, then place in the fridge or freezer. This will keep the edges soft and maintain maximum moisture!

NOTE Both of the cake recipes in this book have a runny batter and long cooking time, so we do not recommend a springform pan. We have found the recipes work best in a high-quality aluminium cake tin. Lower-quality tins may affect cooking times.

NOTE To ensure your cake doesn't stick to the tin, make sure you line your tin with baking paper NOT greaseproof paper. They are not the same thing!

Tigga's VANILLA VELVET CAKE

This is a great alternative to our chocolate mud cake and
has a velvety texture and vanilla flavour. It freezes well,
so can be made in advance and thawed before use.

We always bake our cakes at least a day prior to decorating and
refrigerate them overnight wrapped in cling film. This ensures the
cake is cold before decorating, making it easier to carve and handle.
It's the perfect cake for any Tigga Mac cake hack!

THIS RECIPE WILL YIELD EITHER:

**1 × 20CM ROUND
OR SQUARE CAKE**

**OR 2 × 15CM
ROUND CAKES**

The cake tin needs to be at least 7cm high. Many cake tins are
only 3–4cm high but this recipe and the hacks won't work in a low tin.

PREP TIME – 30 minutes

COOK TIME – 1 hour 10 minutes

You Will Need

125ml canola oil

375g caster sugar

2 teaspoons vanilla extract

1 teaspoon vinegar

300g self-raising flour

1 teaspoon baking powder

½ teaspoon salt

200ml boiling water

2 large eggs

200g unsalted butter

250ml buttermilk

Scan for video tutorial!

1. Preheat the oven to 180°C (160°C fan-forced). Using cooking spray, grease your chosen cake tin (depending on the hack you are creating) and line the base and sides with baking paper.

2. In a mixing bowl combine the canola oil, caster sugar, vanilla extract and vinegar. Set aside.

3. In another bowl combine the flour, baking powder and salt.

4. Carefully measure the boiling water in a heatproof jug and add to the mixing bowl with the oil and sugar. Using a whisk, mix until the sugar has dissolved.

5. Add the dry ingredients to the mixing bowl and whisk until combined. Scrape the sides of the bowl and then mix again for 1 minute.

6. Add the eggs and mix until combined.

7. In a saucepan, melt the butter and remove from the heat. Add to the mixture, then mix until combined.

8. Add the buttermilk and mix until smooth. You may be concerned about the consistency of your batter, but it is meant to be runny! Check out the video for a visual reference.

9. Pour the cake batter into the lined tin.

10. Cover the tin with foil before placing it in the preheated oven. The baking time will vary depending on the size of the cake or cakes you are making and your oven. In our oven, a 20cm vanilla velvet cake takes 1 hour 10 minutes. We suggest setting the timer for 1 hour, then testing the centre of the cake with a skewer. If the skewer does not come out clean, this means your cake is not fully baked. Keep checking at regular intervals until the skewer comes out clean.

11. Once the cake has been removed from the oven, wait 15 minutes before turning it out onto a cooling rack. Wrap the cake in cling film while still warm, then place in the fridge or freezer. This will keep the edges soft and maintain maximum moisture!

NOTE Both of the cake recipes in this book have a runny batter and long cooking time, so we do not recommend a springform pan. We have found the recipes work best in a high-quality aluminium cake tin. Lower-quality tins may affect cooking times.

NOTE To ensure your cake doesn't stick to the tin, make sure you line your tin with baking paper NOT greaseproof paper. They are not the same thing!

Tigga's Buttercream Basics

One of the main obstacles when starting your cake decorating journey is the type of buttercream you use! If your icing is too stiff, it can make your job so much more difficult! The icing can pull at the cake, causing damage and allowing crumbs to be seen.

Knowing which buttercream to use can be overwhelming. There are so many different types out there! Swiss, Italian, French, American, Ermine . . . the possibilities are endless! Our particular recipe is a hybrid version of Swiss and American buttercream.

WE FIND IT'S THE PERFECT SILKY-SMOOTH CONSISTENCY, AND REMAINS SWEET WITHOUT HAVING AN OVERWHELMING BUTTER FLAVOUR

It is perfect for cake decorating, as it is so soft and spreadable but remains sturdy enough for piping details. And it hardens in the fridge for maximum stability when assembling your cake.

Eggs

Normally when making Swiss meringue buttercream you heat the egg whites over a simmering water bath to dissolve your sugar. This process can be quite time consuming and requires extra equipment. We decided to use pasteurised egg whites to streamline the entire process. They are completely safe, as any bacteria has already been killed which eliminates the need for heating. They can be purchased in at your local supermarket! You can use fresh egg whites, but the method will change as you will need to heat the egg whites and sugar to 85°C (185°F) to kill any bacteria.

You are welcome to use your own buttercream recipe or even a store-bought option, but keep in mind when it comes to decorating, a soft and spreadable buttercream (like ours!) will set you up for success!!

Storage

Leftover buttercream can be wrapped in cling film or placed in a microwave-safe container for up to 10 days. To reuse, microwave in short bursts until softened and pop back into the mixer to whip back to a soft, spreadable consistency.

After decorating we recommend popping your cake in the fridge to harden and stabilise, especially if you need to transport your cake to an event.

When it comes time to display your cake, our buttercream is stable at room temperature! At room temperature, our buttercream has a beautiful smooth flavour and a melt-in-the-mouth consistency.

Tigga's BUTTERCREAM

Some of the cakes in this book will not utilise the entire batch of buttercream. Leftover buttercream can be covered with cling film or placed in a microwave-safe container and refrigerated for up to 10 days. To reuse, microwave the buttercream in 10-second bursts until softened, then pop it back into the mixer and whisk to a soft, spreadable consistency. Note that we use icing sugar mixture for this recipe, as pure icing sugar can be lumpy. If you would prefer to use pure icing sugar, ensure to sift before adding.

THIS RECIPE WILL YIELD:

A BIT OVER 1.2KG OF BUTTERCREAM

You Will Need

180ml pasteurised egg whites

300g caster sugar

240g icing sugar mixture

620g unsalted butter

1 teaspoon vanilla extract

Scan for video tutorial!

1 Using an electric stand mixer with a whisk attachment, whisk the egg whites and caster sugar to make a thick meringue. Whisk until the sugar has dissolved and the meringue has reached stiff peaks (about 15 minutes).

2 Turn off the mixer and add the icing sugar mixture to the bowl. Whisk on low until just combined and then increase speed to high until fully incorporated.

3 Soften the butter in the microwave. It should be soft but not melted.

4 Add the butter and vanilla extract to the bowl and beat for 10 minutes. (Optional: Switch your whisk attachment for a paddle attachment to beat out air bubbles and achieve a smoother consistency.) The buttercream is now ready to use!

Chocolate buttercream: Some of our hacks use brown buttercream and for this you can use brown gel colouring. Alternatively, you can make chocolate buttercream! To do this, simply use our dark chocolate ganache (see page 16). Ensuring your ganache is at a spreadable consistency, whip the ganache through the finished buttercream a spoonful at a time until you reach the desired colour and taste!

DARK CHOCOLATE GANACHE

Ganache is a type of filling, glaze or sauce that combines melted chocolate and cream. It is extremely versatile and absolutely delicious!

The thing we love most about ganache is that it will set firm at room temperature, making it the perfect choice for tiered and tall or layered cakes. It is stable at room temperature for days and extremely sturdy. Bonus: it's not sugary!

We have included our ganache recipe to give you another filling option for your cakes and it can also be added to our buttercream recipe to make it chocolate flavoured (see page 15).

You Will Need

500g dark chocolate
300ml thickened or double cream

1 Break the dark chocolate into a large microwave-safe bowl. Set aside.

2 Heat the thickened cream in a saucepan over low heat until just starting to bubble – it will boil over if left unattended, so watch it closely! Remove from the heat.

3 Carefully pour the hot cream over the chocolate and stir until combined.

4 If the ganache still has some lumps of chocolate in it, place the bowl in the microwave and heat in 30-second bursts until the chocolate has melted. Stir to combine, then set aside until cooled.

5 Cover the bowl with cling film and leave at room temperature until set (at least 4 hours). To use, return the ganache to the microwave and heat for 30-second bursts until soft and spreadable.

MARSHMALLOW EYES

You will see that many of the cake hacks in this book have marshmallow eyes. They are simple to create and incredibly effective! They are also really yummy!

Please keep in mind if you are making your cake in advance, the coating on the M&M's can run in the fridge. So if you are decorating your cake the day before, we would recommend adding your eyes last, before popping it on display!

You Will Need

1 white marshmallow (cut in half)
2 brown M&M's

1 Cut Marshmallow

Take one marshmallow and carefully cut it in half. You will now have two equal-sized round pieces. By cutting it in half you have now created a sticky side on each piece of marshmallow.

2 Stick on M&M's

Grab your brown M&M's and stick them onto the centre of the sticky side of both of your marshmallows. That's all there is to it! Now using some buttercream as glue, you can attach the eyes onto the face of your cake character!

EDIBLE MOSS

This moss is such an easy recipe and it's the perfect addition to any cake scene! Edible moss is used in Fairy Hill House (page 55), Train Tunnel (page 95) and Let's Go Camping (page 193).

You Will Need

1 egg

1 teaspoon honey

1 tablespoon sugar

40g plain flour

1¼ teaspoons baking powder

green gel food colouring

yellow gel food colouring

brown gel food colouring

1. In a small microwave-safe bowl, mix the egg, honey and sugar until combined.

2. In a separate bowl, combine the flour and baking powder, then add this to the egg mixture. Mix thoroughly for at least 1 minute. Overmixing is key for your moss to work!

3. Gradually mix in green and yellow colouring with a dash of brown to achieve a deep moss colour, bearing in mind the colour will brighten up once cooked.

4. Microwave for 1 minute. Set aside to cool.

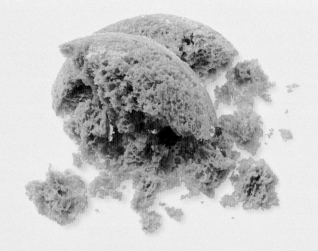

HOW TO FILL A PIPING BAG

It may sound easy but one of the most common questions I receive is, 'How do I fill a piping bag correctly?' From holding the bag incorrectly to overfilling, the last thing you want is to have your hands and workspace covered in buttercream! Rest assured, once you have nailed the correct technique, it will become second nature!

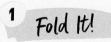

1 Fold It!

Fold over the top of your piping bag to create a cuff.

2 Cut It!

Without piping tip: You just need to cut the end of the bag off. The size of the hole that you cut will really depend on what you are using it for. For finer details, a smaller hole will be required. If you are piping over your entire cake, a larger hole is needed.

With piping tip: Pop your chosen piping tip into the bag and trim the end so about one-third of the tip is sticking out. Make sure your hole isn't too big, as this can cause the piping tip to burst out through the hole when piping!

3 Hold It!

To hold the bag, place your non-dominant hand inside the cuff. Use your fingers to hold the bag open.

4 Fill It!

Using your other hand, spoon in the buttercream. Fill the bag no more than two-thirds full. If you are finding this step difficult or uncomfortable you can also place the bag into a tall glass and fold the cuff over the rim. The glass will hold the bag open for you!

5 Twist It!

Now your bag is full, unfold the cuff and hold the bag closed with one hand. Using your other hand, press the buttercream down towards the bottom of the bag. Twist the bag closed where the buttercream ends. For extra security, you can use a rubber band to keep your bag closed.

6 Burp It!

Before piping onto your cake, I would suggest burping the bag. This just means squeezing a small amount of buttercream out of the bag and back into your bowl, removing any air that may be trapped in there. Now you're ready to pipe!

WHIMSICAL & WONDERFUL

Enter a world of whimsy and wonder, where the only
limit is your imagination. If colour and magic is your kind
of thing, what are you waiting for? Step right in!

As a child I spent hours writing stories about fairies, unicorns and
rainbows, complete with detailed illustrations. I absolutely loved
spending time daydreaming about these wonderful, creative worlds.

Daydreaming is something we could all spend more time doing and
this chapter gives everyone the chance to explore their imaginations!

The magic behind these hacks is that whilst you are given
suggested ideas, each hack can be adapted to be completely
unique and personalised for YOU! Step outside the box.

We encourage you to choose your favourite colours and add
your own special touches to bring these cakes to life!

RAINBOW CAKE

The rainbow cake will always hold a special place in my heart as it was the first hack I ever attempted! The cleverness of this hack is in its versatility, as it suits any age and any type of celebration. It is by far one of the easiest cakes to make and yet the end result is so effective. It's the perfect cake for beginners and also a great one to include little helpers, who love sorting the colours and popping on those fluffy marshmallow clouds. Give it a go and find the magic at the end of the rainbow!

You Will Need

30cm round cake board

1 piping bag

~~~

1 20cm round cake (see pages 10–13)

1 batch Tigga's buttercream (see page 15)

1 380g packet Smarties or M&M's, sorted into colours

1 180g packet white marshmallows

100s & 1000s or sprinkles

Cut the Cake!

Okie dokie, let's go over the rainbow! Following the cutting guide, cut your cake in half, directly down the middle.

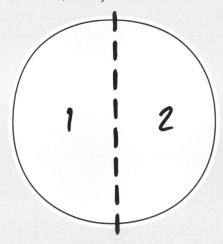

1 Assembly

Spread a little buttercream on the cake board where the base of your rainbow will sit. This will be the glue that stops the cake from moving around while you are decorating it. Sandwich the 2 cake halves together with a layer of buttercream and stick the cake to the board so it is standing upright.

Yay! You have your rainbow shape!

2 Buttercream Time

Using a palette knife, coat the entire cake in white buttercream. It doesn't need to be perfect as you will be covering the entire cake in rainbow sweets. No crumb coat required!

Tigga's Tips ★
Buy an extra bag of M&M's in case you need more of a particular colour.

3 Add Your Colour

It's RAINBOW time! Arrange the Smarties or M&M's over the cake in coloured rows, following the shape of the rainbow. Continue until the entire cake is covered.

WHIMSICAL & WONDERFUL

Easy as!

4 Clouds

Now you've coloured the rainbow, dip one end of each marshmallow into the remaining buttercream and stick them to the base of the cake to create a cloud effect.

5 Complete Clouds

Fill a piping bag with buttercream and cut a 1cm hole in the end. Pipe white 'blobs' among the marshmallows to complete the clouds.

6 Finishing Touches

Scatter some sprinkles or 100s & 1000s over the buttercream in the clouds and – BAM! – you've got yourself a gorgeous rainbow cake.

LOVE HEART CAKE

*easy peasy!

This cake requires no occasion. Yes, it works for birthdays, anniversaries, engagements and Valentine's Day. Of course, every day should be a celebration of love and the perfect way to show that love is with cake!

You Will Need

30cm round cake board

1 20cm round cake (see pages 10–13)
1 batch Tigga's buttercream (see page 15)
100s & 1000s or sprinkles

Cut the Cake!

Okie dokie, the key to this hack is turning a round cake into a heart shape. Start by pressing a ruler horizontally across the centre of the cake to mark a line. Repeat this vertically. The cake should now be marked with a cross, showing 4 even quarters. Follow the cutting guide and neatly cut away the rounded edge of the left-hand quarter in one movement, then repeat with the right-hand quarter. Lastly, cut a small triangle from the top of the cake. You will now have a main cake, 2 semicircular pieces and a small triangle offcut.

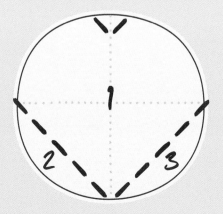

1 Assembly

Let's put the pieces together! Spread a little buttercream on the cake board where the cake will sit. This will be the glue that stops the cake from moving around while you are decorating it. Stick the large cake piece to the board.

2 Heart Shape

This next part is really clever! To finish the heart shape, attach pieces 2 and 3 to the top of the cake with buttercream, pressing firmly. Don't be afraid to really squash these pieces on to make sure they stay put.

Really squash them on so they stay put!

WHIMSICAL & WONDERFUL

3 Buttercream Time

Coat the entire cake in a crumb coat of buttercream, smoothing it with a palette knife. For extra-smooth sides, you can use a cake scraper. Chill the cake in the fridge for 10 minutes or until firm.

Then, add a second coat of buttercream, once again smoothing it with a palette knife and a scraper. You are now ready for the 100s & 1000s or sprinkles!

4 Finishing Touches

This is the best part so don't be afraid to make some mess! Pour the 100s & 1000s or sprinkles into a bowl. Using your hands, carefully pat them onto the cake to completely cover the top and sides. Carefully pick up the cake and tap lightly on the board to allow any excess to fall back into the bowl. There you have it! Your cake is finished. Take a moment to step back and admire your work! Amazing job.

You're an absolute

HEARTSTOPPER!

BIRTHDAY BUTTERFLY

medium!

It's hard not to be captivated by a butterfly's wings and entranced by the incredible patterns created by nature. The best thing about the Birthday Butterfly cake is that every butterfly is unique. Bring on the colour and design your own flying masterpiece – we have chosen pink here for the wings, but the sky is your limit!

You Will Need

30cm round cake board

1 piping bag

1 pipe cleaner

~~~~~~

1 20cm round cake (see pages 10–13)

1 batch Tigga's buttercream (see page 15)

green gel food colouring

pink gel food colouring

2 edible icing eyeballs

1 340g packet Smarties

2 round coloured biscuits

Cut the Cake!

Okie dokie, let's fly! Following the cutting guide, cut the cake in half to make the wings. Next, cut out 2 small triangles from the centre of the straight side of each wing. You won't be using these offcuts, so feel free to eat them!

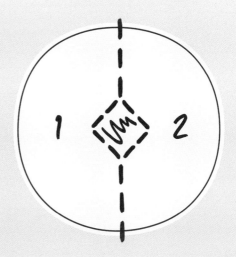

1 Colour

First make the coloured buttercream – remember to add the food colouring a little at a time until you are happy with the result. Scoop 55g of buttercream into a small bowl and colour it green. Colour the remaining buttercream pink.

2 Assembly

Spread a little buttercream on the cake board where the cake will sit. This will be the glue that stops the cake from moving around while you are decorating it. Assemble the butterfly by turning the 'wings' around so the curved edges meet in the middle and stick them to the board.

3 Buttercream Time

Coat the entire cake in a crumb coat of pink buttercream, smoothing it with a palette knife. For extra-smooth sides, you can use a cake scraper. Chill the cake in the fridge for 10 minutes or until firm. Add a second coat of pink buttercream, once again smoothing it out with a palette knife and a scraper.

4 Body

Fill a piping bag with the green buttercream and cut a 1cm hole in the end. To make the body, pipe out a swirly line down the centre of the butterfly. Next, pop on the edible eyes.

5 Finishing Touches

Now it's time to let your imagination fly! Place a biscuit coloured-side up on each lower wing. Decorate the wings in pretty patterns with Smarties. Finally, to make the antennae, cut the pipe cleaner in half, twist the ends and poke them into the head. Snap some pics and smile bright, your Birthday Butterfly is ready to take flight!

Tigga's Tips ★
On a piece of baking paper, trace around your cake pieces before you begin decorating. You can use this as a template to practise your wing pattern designs.

YOU ARE MY SUNSHINE

* medium!

This cake will warm you up from the inside out! Unlike our other cakes where we cut them before adding the buttercream, our sunshine cake uses a 'cake-top forward' technique. This means you will be covering the cake with buttercream before slicing a small portion off one side and then standing it up so the top faces forward. This hack gives you the chance to get crafty and can be adapted to become a flower by swapping the rays for petals!

You Will Need

25cm round cake board

baking paper

coloured card

~~~

1 20cm round cake (see pages 10–13)

1 batch Tigga's buttercream (see page 15)

yellow gel food colouring

2 marshmallow eyes (see page 17)

1 pink marshmallow

1 white marshmallow

Scan for video tutorial!

Cut the Cake!

Okie dokie, for this hack, cut the cake in a later step rather than right at the start. Come back here when you get to Step 3.

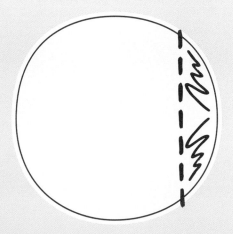

1 Colour

First make the coloured buttercream – remember to add the food colouring a little at a time until you are happy with the result. Colour the buttercream yellow. Measure out about one-third of the buttercream and set it aside (this is used to coat the back of the cake later).

2 Buttercream Time

Spread a little buttercream on the cake board to secure your cake temporarily. This will be the glue that stops the cake from moving around while you apply the crumb coat and are decorating it. Coat the cake in a crumb coat of buttercream, smoothing it with a palette knife. For extra-smooth sides, you can use a cake scraper. Chill in the fridge for 10 minutes or until firm.

When ready, add a second coat of yellow buttercream, once again smoothing it out with a palette knife and a scraper. Chill the cake in the fridge for another 10 minutes or until firm.

WHIMSICAL & WONDERFUL

3 Stand It Up

Check your cake is very cold and the buttercream has set hard, then follow the cutting guide and slice the side off your cake. You don't need this offcut so feel free to eat it or keep it aside for later and serve it with the rest of the cake!

Tigga's Tips ★
To help with the removal of your cake from the board, simply run a knife around the base of the cake.

Now, get ready, it's time for the hard part! First, have a sheet of baking paper ready alongside the cake board. Then, slide a palette knife underneath the cake and transfer the cake from the board to the baking paper.

Following that, clean the cake board and spread a little of the reserved buttercream across the centre of the board. Carefully stand the cake on the board with the cut edge down and the cake top forward, then pop it back into the fridge for another 10 minutes to chill.

4 Complete Coverage

You'll notice the back of the cake is naked! Let's cover it up! Using a palette knife, coat the back in the reserved buttercream and smooth with a palette knife and cake scraper.

No more naked cake!

Keep going until the entire cake is covered and as smooth as possible. This is important before you start creating your sunny face.

5 Happy Face

Place the marshmallow eyes on the front of the cake. Use a pink marshmallow cut in half for rosy cheeks. For the mouth, use a slice of white marshmallow.

6 Getting Crafty

Now it's time to make your sun SHINE! Using coloured card, cut out triangle shapes for the sun's rays. Place them on the cake, carefully pushing them into the buttercream to make sure they stay put.

Tigga's Tips ★ When attaching your sun's rays, don't be afraid to overlap them slightly to achieve the perfect fit!

This is the reverse side. Notice how the bottom corners overlap and are evenly spaced out. Take time with your rays to get the look you want!

Wow! Look at that sun shining so bright! Time to show it off and spread the sunshine.

BORN TO UNICORN

it's a challenge!

There is no doubt about it, the unicorn craze is here to stay!
And now you can create your own magical unicorn at home.
Better still, you can give your unicorn its very own name! Check out
our fun unicorn name game at the end of this hack to find out yours.

You Will Need

25cm round cake board

1 soft bristle paint brush

cling film

3 piping bags

1 large star tip nozzle

~~~

1 20cm round cake (see pages 10–13)

1 batch Tigga's buttercream (see page 15)

pink gel food colouring

yellow gel food colouring

purple gel food colouring

1 pink wafer

2 marshmallow eyes (see page 17)

2 brown M&M's

edible gold shimmer

1 ice-cream cone

sprinkles

edible glitter

Cut the Cake!

Okie dokie, first up, cut the cake following
the cutting guide. Start with the largest
vertical off-centre cut, followed by the
2 smaller horizontal cuts. You will end up
with 4 pieces: (1) the head, (2) the nose,
and (3) and (4) the ears. Carefully trim down
the sides of piece 1 to square off the head.
Any leftover cake is yours to snack on!

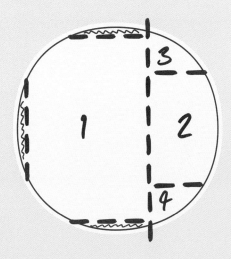

1 Colour

Get ready for some colour magic! First make the coloured buttercream – remember to add the food colouring a little at a time until you are happy with the result. Take 2 bowls and scoop 105g of buttercream into each one, then colour one pink and the other yellow. Scoop 320g of buttercream into a third bowl and colour it purple. Leave the remaining buttercream in its original bowl – it stays white.

2 Assembly

Spread a little white buttercream on the cake board where the cake will sit. This will be the glue that stops the cake from moving around while you are decorating it. Stand the head piece (1) upright on the board.

Next, secure the nose (2) upright against the head using buttercream. Keep pieces 3 and 4 aside for ears. Chill the cake in the fridge for 10 minutes or until firm.

WHIMSICAL & WONDERFUL

3 Shaping

Using a small serrated knife, carefully round off the edges of the nose to remove sharp corners.

4 Buttercream Time

First up, crumb coat time. Fill a piping bag with white buttercream and roughly pipe over the head of the unicorn. Smooth using a palette knife. Keep the piping bag handy for later use. Fill a second piping bag with purple buttercream and pipe over the nose, once again smoothing with a palette knife. Chill in the fridge for 10 minutes or until firm.

When ready, add a second coat of both buttercream colours, once again smoothing it with a palette knife and a scraper.

5   Ears

For the unicorn's ears, stick cake pieces 3 and 4 on top of the head with buttercream. Chill for 10 minutes or until firm before continuing. Once the ears feel firm enough, use the piping bag to pipe over them using white buttercream. Smooth out with a palette knife.

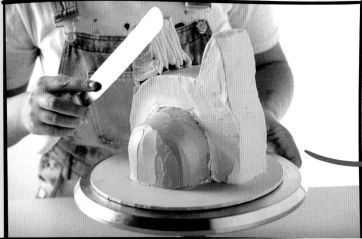

To finish off the ears, cut the wafer in half diagonally to create 2 triangles and place one on the front of each ear.

6   Eyes

Stick the marshmallow eyes on the front of the head.

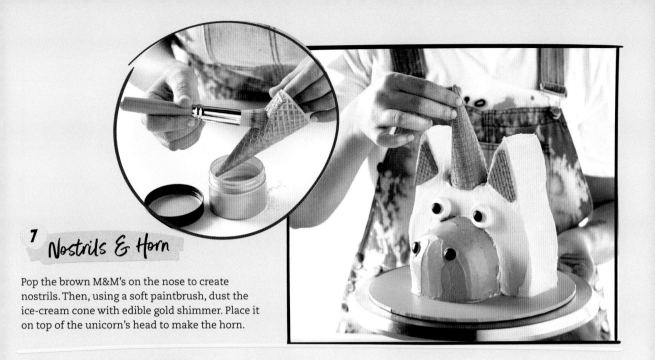

7 Nostrils & Horn

Pop the brown M&M's on the nose to create nostrils. Then, using a soft paintbrush, dust the ice-cream cone with edible gold shimmer. Place it on top of the unicorn's head to make the horn.

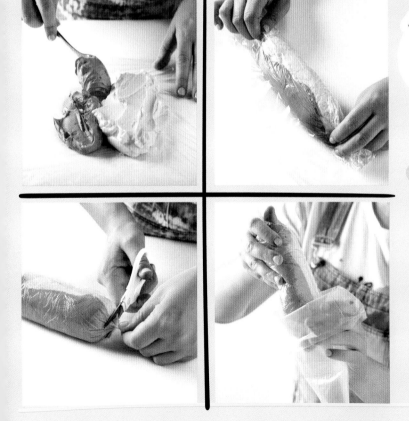

Tigga's Tips ★

Make extra rainbow buttercream and use the multicolour piping technique for matching unicorn cupcakes!

8 Prep for the Mane

Time to bring on the rainbow magic! Prepare your piping bag by popping in the star tip nozzle. Set aside. Next up, place a 40cm piece of cling film on your bench. Spoon the pink and yellow buttercream onto the cling film, side by side. Roll up the cling film to create a buttercream 'sausage' and twist the ends, then cut off the excess cling film at one end. Put the buttercream 'sausage', cut-end down, into the prepared piping bag.

9 The Mane Event

Pipe the multicoloured buttercream around and in front of the horn to create a fringe.

Then, pipe behind the ears and continue down and around one side of the head, bringing the mane down to the board.

Finally, add some sprinkles and edible glitter to your mane and . . .

WOAH! Pure MAGIC!

NAME YOUR UNICORN

Want a magical name for your creation? Simply select the first letter of your name and your birthday month. *Ta da!*

Our unicorn names are *Clover Fire Storm* and *Spirit Cotton Tail!*

A * Sparkle   G * Cuddly   N * Fluffy   U * Rainbow
B * Magical   H * Golden   O * Candy   V * Sprinkle
C * Twinkle   I * Whacky   P * Lucky   W * Bright
D * Lightning   J * Diamond   Q * Sassy   X * Shiny
E * Dancing   K * Spirit   R * Midnight   Y * Sunset
F * Bubbly   L * Mystical   S * Dizzy   Z * Dreamy
                 M * Enchanted   T * Clover

JANUARY   **MAY**   **SEPTEMBER**
Twinkle Toes   Lemon Drop   Passion Pop

FEBRUARY   **JUNE**   **OCTOBER**
Moon Wing   Glitter Fart   Giggle Pants

MARCH   **JULY**   **NOVEMBER**
Sky Dancer   Sugar Cookie   Baby Face

APRIL   **AUGUST**   **DECEMBER**
Pop Tart   Cotton Tail   Fire Storm

MAGICAL MERMAID TAIL

it's a challenge!

Follow the siren song and discover a world of mermaid magic! In just a few simple steps you can transform an ordinary round cake into a mermaid's tail. My favourite part of this hack is the scales – so simple but so effective!

You Will Need

25cm × 45cm large rectangular cake board

3 piping bags

~~~

1 20cm round cake (see pages 10–13)

1 batch Tigga's buttercream (see page 15)

pink gel food colouring

purple gel food colouring

aqua gel food colouring

sprinkles

Scan for video tutorial!

Cut the Cake!

Okie dokie, it's time to make a splash! First up, cut the cake following the cutting guide, starting with the 2 largest cuts. You will end up with 3 large pieces and 3 small pieces. You will need all of them for this hack, so no snacking!

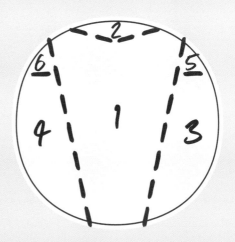

1 Colour

First make the coloured buttercream – you need 3 colours for the mermaid's tail. Remember to add the food colouring a little at a time until you are happy with the result. To start, scoop 215g of buttercream into a bowl and add pink gel food colouring. Divide the remaining buttercream between 2 bowls and colour one purple and the other aqua.

2 Assembly

The largest cake piece (1) is the main part of the mermaid's tail, and pieces 3 and 4 are the tail fins. Spread a little buttercream on the cake board where the cake will sit. This will be the glue that stops the cake from moving around while you are decorating it. Attach piece 1 to the board, leaving space below for the fins. Next up, stick piece 2 on the bottom of the tail to create a point. Attach pieces 3 and 4 to the end of your tail, with the pointy ends facing down – these are the fins. Place the final pieces, 5 and 6, at the top of the tail to complete the shape.

3 Buttercream Time

Cover the main portion of the tail in purple buttercream and the fins in aqua, smoothing with a palette knife and a cake scraper. Chill in the fridge for 10 minutes or until firm.

WHIMSICAL & WONDERFUL

4 Scales

Put the pink, purple and aqua buttercream in 3 separate piping bags. Cut the tip off each piping bag to give a 1cm opening. Starting from the bottom of the tail (just above the fins), pipe small blobs of buttercream in a horizontal line across the tail, alternating colours randomly.

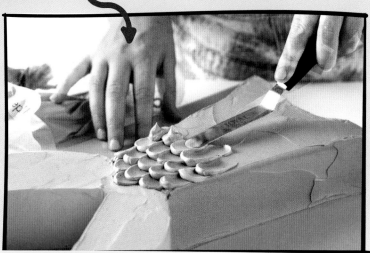

Then, lightly smear each blob in an upward direction with a small palette or butter knife to create the scales. Make sure you clean the knife when you change colours by scraping any excess buttercream off on the edge of a bowl and wiping the knife clean with a cloth.

5 Tail Details

Use the aqua buttercream to pipe lines across the top of the mermaid's tail and over the fins to create a textured look. Add something extra to your mermaid's tail with sprinkles!

Sprinkle some fairy dust and enter a magical world of your own making! Yes, we give you the guide and the structure, but YOU are the magic ingredient. Your ideas and decorations will make this house a home! We use a grass tip nozzle here, but if you don't have one just use the star tip nozzle for both the grass and the house. The result will still be magical!

You Will Need

30cm round cake board

3 piping bags

1 star tip nozzle

1 grass tip nozzle (optional)

~~~

1 20cm round cake (see pages 10–13)

1 batch Tigga's buttercream (see page 15)

brown gel food colouring

green gel food colouring

5 round coloured biscuits
(we used 1 pink and 4 yellow)

1 30g Cadbury Flake

1 16g packet icing flowers

edible glitter

1 batch edible moss (see page 18)

Cut the Cake!

Okie dokie, cut the cake in half, slightly off centre.

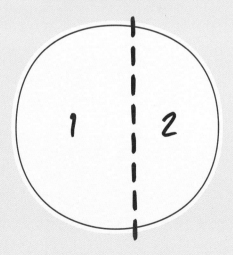

1 Colour

Time to make the coloured buttercream – remember to add the food colouring a little at a time until you are happy with the result. Scoop 320g of buttercream into a bowl and colour it dark brown. Colour the remaining buttercream grass green.

2 Assembly

Spread a little buttercream on the cake board where the cake will sit. This will be the glue that stops the cake from moving around while you are decorating it. Then, sandwich the 2 cake pieces together with some buttercream and stand them upright on the cake board. The taller side is the front of the house.

3 Shaping

Using a sharp knife, carve the back of the cake away to achieve a rounded finish. Don't throw away (or eat) these offcuts! To complete the shape of the hill, use buttercream to attach the offcuts to the back and sides of your cake. Don't be afraid to really squish them on! Chill the cake in the fridge for 10 minutes or until set.

Keep those offcuts!

WHIMSICAL & WONDERFUL

Remember to leave a space for the path!

4 Buttercream Time

Fill a piping bag with green buttercream and cover the entire chilled cake in a crumb coat, smoothing with a palette knife. The buttercream doesn't have to be neat, as you will be piping over it in the next step. Lastly, spread a thin layer of green buttercream around the house and onto the board, leaving a gap where the path will be. Pop the cake back in the fridge to chill for 10 minutes until the buttercream is firm.

5 Front of House

Place the star tip nozzle into a piping bag and fill with brown buttercream. Pipe vertical lines up the entire front of the cake. This will give the fairy house a wooden look.

6 Doors & Windows

It's not a house without doors and windows! For the door, push a pink biscuit onto the front of the house. Place 2 yellow biscuits either side of the door for windows (we used yellow biscuits to give the illusion there are lights on inside the house!). Add another yellow biscuit 'window' to the back of the fairy house.

To complete the look, pipe frames around all 3 windows and the door with brown buttercream.

7 Path

Create a path by piping the remaining brown buttercream onto the board and smooth it out using a palette knife. Break a yellow biscuit into small pieces and press these into the buttercream to create a paved mosaic path.

8 Grass

Now it is time to create the grass for your hill! Using a separate piping bag, pop in a grass tip nozzle (if you have one, otherwise use a star tip nozzle) and fill with green buttercream. Start by piping a border of grass across the top of the cake and around the base. Keep piping until the back of the cake is covered. Lastly, pipe a grassy border along the path. This grass piping is time consuming, but the end result is worth it!

Tigga's Tips ★

When creating your grass effect, make sure your buttercream isn't too soft and warm. Also, if you find during piping that the look of your grass is becoming messy and less defined, simply clean off your nozzle and resume piping!

9 Extra Detail

Now it's time to add some magic little details! For the chimney, cut the chocolate flake in half and place half a flake on top of the house on one side. Break the other half of the chocolate flake into pieces and line the path.

10 Magic Moss

Now it's time for the moss! Let's use it! Using your hands, pull the moss apart into small pieces. Place these all around the cake and cake board.

11 Finishing Touches

Place icing flowers all around the house and, lastly, add some edible glitter as your fairy dust! Sprinkle it everywhere your fairy has been and make a wish.

WHIMSICAL & WONDERFUL

FARMYARD FRIENDS

Grab your wellies and overalls . . . we are heading to the farm!

There is nothing quite like seeing the fascination on a child's face the first time they visit a farm. The sounds, smells and sights create a sense of curiosity and wonder, at any age!

You don't have to have experienced farms in real life to feel a sense of nostalgia around farm animals. From nursery rhymes to learning animal sounds, Farmyard Friends reflects a part of everyone's childhood experience.

Our farmyard hacks are total crowd-pleasers, ranging from the simple Woolly Sheep – the perfect cake for beginners – to the more advanced Farm Dog.

Whilst we have created our own versions of farmyard friends, keep in mind they are totally adaptable! By changing the colours, these cute characters can be adapted to reflect any favourite TV animal character or even a beloved family pet!

WOOLLY SHEEP

easy peasy!

This woolly sheep is BAAAAA-UTIFUL! The perfect cake for beginners as there is no carving or cutting involved. It's just a matter of coating your cake in delicious buttercream and covering this sheep in fluffy marshmallow wool!

You Will Need

25cm round cake board

1 piping bag

1 20cm round cake (see pages 10–13)
1 batch Tigga's buttercream (see page 15)
28 white marshmallows
1 giant white marshmallow
1 pink marshmallow
2 brown M&M's
pink sprinkles

Cut the Cake!

Okie dokie, no need to cut anything – all you need is the round cake then let's cracking. How easy is that?!

No need to cut this one!

1 Assembly

Spread a little buttercream on the cake board where the cake will sit. This will be the glue that stops the cake moving around while you are decorating it.

2 Buttercream Time

Coat the entire cake in a crumb coat of buttercream, smoothing it with a palette knife. For extra-smooth sides, you can use a cake scraper. Chill the cake in the fridge for 10 minutes or until firm. Add a second coat of buttercream, once again smoothing it with a palette knife and a scraper. You now have a round white cake – the sheep's head!

3 Ears

Cut a giant white marshmallow in half to create 2 ovals. Place your sprinkles into a small bowl and dip the sticky side of the oval marshmallows into the pink sprinkles. Place the 2 ears on either side of the cake.

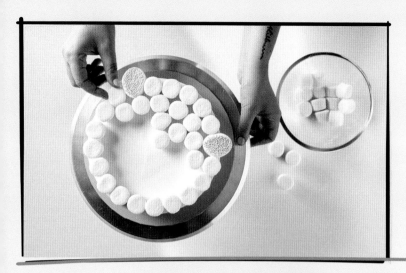

4 Wool

Place white marshmallows along the top of the cake until they touch the ears, then continue adding them until you complete the border. Place more white marshmallows to the top half of the face, as shown.

5 Face

Place the 2 brown M&M's for the eyes. Cut a pink marshmallow into a triangle and pop it on for the nose.

6 Border

Feelin' fancy? Use the leftover buttercream to pipe a border around the base of your cake! That's all there is to it: one adorable Woolly Sheep!

CHEEKY CHICK

medium!

I challenge you to look at the Cheeky Chick and not feel warm and fuzzy inside! From the coconut feathers to the crunchy chocolate nest, this chick is an eggs-tremely egg-cellent addition to any celebration!

You Will Need

30cm round cake board

1 piping bag

baking paper

2 15cm round cakes (see pages 10–13)

1 batch Tigga's buttercream (see page 15)

yellow gel food colouring

80g desiccated coconut

1 tablespoon water

2 ice cream wafers

2 marshmallow eyes (see page 17)

2 orange M&M's

200g milk or dark chocolate

2 100g packet fried dried noodles

chocolate eggs

Cut the Cake!

Okie dokie, no need to cut anything at the start, but there will be some cutting involved from Step 3.

No need to cut the cakes just yet!

1 Colour

Colour all of your buttercream yellow – remember to add the food colouring a little at a time until you are happy with the result.

2 Prep the Feathers

Place 80g of desiccated coconut into a large bowl. Squeeze 2–3 drops of yellow gel colouring into a small bowl with 1 tablespoon of water. Stir together and then pour into the coconut. Mix together until all the coconut is yellow. Set aside.

3 Stacking

Now we need to do some careful cutting and stacking. First, cut both cakes in half horizontally, creating 4 layers. Then, stack all 4 layers on top of each other with a generous layer of buttercream between each one. Chill the cake in the fridge for 10 minutes or until firm.

4 Wings

Using a sharp knife or scissors, cut the corners off the wafers to form a wing shape. Coat both wafers in yellow buttercream and yellow coconut, then place them on baking paper and chill in the fridge to set.

5 Carving

To make the shape of your chick, you need to round off the top of the cake. Using a sharp serrated knife, carefully carve the top edges of the cake away in a downward motion until you have achieved a rounded shape. Feel free to eat the offcuts!

6 Buttercream Time

Using a palette knife, cover the entire cake in yellow buttercream. This is the crumb coat. It doesn't have to be perfect as you will be covering it! Chill in the fridge for 10 minutes or until firm. Add a second coat of buttercream, once again smoothing it with a palette knife.

7 Feathers

Using your hands, coat the entire cake in the yellow coconut feathers that you prepared earlier.

Tigga's Tips ★

Not a fan of coconut? The cheeky chick will look just as cute with textured buttercream or by piping with a star or grass tip nozzle.

8 Details

Fill a piping bag with yellow buttercream and cut a 1cm hole in the end. Pipe some 'hair' onto the top of the chick's head. Attach the wings to the sides of your cake using buttercream.

Then, with a small amount of buttercream, stick the marshmallow eyes on. Lastly, press your 2 orange M&M's into the cake to form a beak.

FARMYARD FRIENDS

9 Nest

Melt down the chocolate in a bowl in 30-second bursts in the microwave. Place the noodles into the melted chocolate and mix to coat the noodles.

Now, carefully spoon your chocolate-coated noodles around your chick to create the nest.

10 Finishing Touches

Scatter your eggs onto the nest and chill in the fridge for 10 minutes to set the chocolate. Voila! One cheeky, cheery, chirpy chick!

MUDDY PARTY PIG

*medium!

Things are about to get MESSY! My favourite part
of this hack is applying the MUD at the end.
It really brings it all together. It's just FUN!

You Will Need

25cm round cake board

1 piping bag

party hat

~~~

1 20cm round cake (see pages 10–13)

1 batch Tigga's buttercream (see page 15)

pink gel food colouring

2 pink wafers

2 brown M&M's or chocolate buttons

2 marshmallow eyes (see page 17)

1 batch dark chocolate ganache
(see page 16)

Cut the Cake!

Okie dokie, cut the cake into 4 pieces
as shown. Start with the longest
cut, followed by the 2 smaller cuts.
You will end up with 4 pieces: the
head (1), snout (2) and ears (3 and 4).

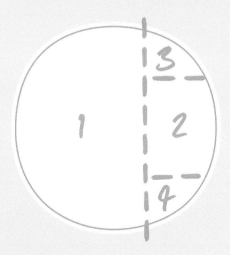

1 Colour

Are you ready to get messy? LET'S GO! Colour the buttercream pink – remember to add the food colouring a little at a time until you are happy with the result.

2 Assembly

Spread a little buttercream on the cake board where the cake will sit. This will be the glue that stops the cake from moving around while you are decorating it. Stand the head piece (1) upright on the board.

Once you've stuck the head to the board, attach the snout (2) to the front of the head using buttercream.

3 Shaping

Using a small serrated knife, carefully round off the edges of the snout to remove sharp corners.

4 Buttercream Time

First up, let's do a crumb coat. Fill a piping bag with the pink buttercream and cut a hole in the end. Roughly pipe buttercream over the entire cake and smooth out using a palette knife. Chill in the fridge for 10 minutes or until set.

Next, add a second coat of buttercream, once again smoothing it with a palette knife.

5 Add Ears

Ensuring there is enough room for the party hat, pop on pieces 3 and 4, the pig's ears, pointing them outwards, using buttercream as the glue. Chill the cake in the fridge for 5–10 minutes to help the buttercream set. This will help make the next step easier.

Now, cover the ears in pink buttercream using the piping bag and palette knife as before.

Then, use a knife to cut the pink wafer biscuits into triangles and place one on the front of each ear.

6 Eyes & Nose

Place the M&M's on the front of the snout for the nostrils. Add the marshmallow eyes.

7 Get Muddy

Warm the chocolate ganache in the microwave in short bursts until soft and spreadable, resembling mud. Place in a piping bag and pipe some mud over the cake board. Use a palette knife to spread out the ganache, making a muddy puddle. Pipe splatters on your pig's snout and over the ear to complete the look.

8 Party Hat

Add a colourful hat and your pig is ready to

PARTY!!!

FLUFFY HIGHLAND COW

it's a challenge!

MOOOOOOOVE on over because the Fluffy Highland Cow has arrived! This hack is slightly more time consuming, but the end result is worth it. The horns, the piped buttercream and those biscuit ears create the most adorable cow you could ever imagine!

You Will Need

25cm round cake board

2 piping bags

1 star tip nozzle

～～～

1 20cm round cake (see pages 10–13)

1 batch Tigga's buttercream (see page 15)

½ batch dark chocolate ganache (see page 16)

pink gel food colouring

1 250g packet round chocolate biscuits

2 marshmallow eyes (see page 17)

2 brown M&M's

1 giant white marshmallow

Cut the Cake!

Okie dokie, let's get mooooooooving! Cut the cake to end up with 2 small offcuts and 2 main pieces – the head (1) and the nose (2). Feel free to snack on the offcuts, as you won't need them!

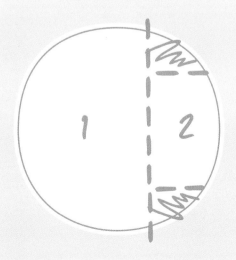

1 Colour

For this cake, you will need 3 colours: pale pink, light brown and dark brown. To start, place 320g of buttercream into a bowl and colour it pale pink. Place another 320g of buttercream in a separate bowl and colour it light brown by stirring through a small amount of chocolate ganache. Then colour the remaining buttercream dark brown by stirring through more chocolate ganache until you have reached the desired colour.

2 Assembly

Spread a little buttercream on the cake board where the cake will sit. This will be the glue that stops the cake from moving around while you are decorating it. Stand the main head piece (1) upright on the board.

Next, stick the nose piece (2) onto the front of your cake using buttercream.

3 Shaping

Using a small serrated knife, carefully round off the edges of the nose piece to remove sharp corners.

4 Buttercream Time

Now the cake is assembled, it's time to get decorating! First up, the crumb coat. Fill a piping bag with 215g of dark-brown buttercream (you will have some spare that will be used later). Cut the tip off the bag to give a 1cm opening. Roughly pipe buttercream over the head of the cow, then smooth it out with a palette knife. It doesn't have to be perfect as you will be piping the cow's fluffy hair over the top. Empty any excess buttercream into your bowl and keep the piping bag aside for later use.

Now, fill a second piping bag with the pink buttercream and pipe over the nose, once again smoothing with a palette knife. Chill the cake in the fridge for 10 minutes or until firm. Apply a second coat of pink buttercream to the nose and smooth out with a palette knife.

5

Fluffy Cow

Place the star tip nozzle in the empty dark-brown buttercream piping bag and refill the bag. You may need to cut a larger hole in the piping bag to allow for the nozzle. Pipe buttercream over the entire head to create your fluffy cow. Keep the piping bag handy for the next step.

6

Ears

The biscuits will become the cow's ears. Using a small, sharp knife, carefully carve the biscuits into shape. Push the biscuits firmly into the sides of the head.

Next, pipe dark-brown buttercream over the back of the ears and around the outer edge. Chill in the fridge for 10 minutes or until firm.

7 Eyes & Nostrils

Place the marshmallow eyes on the front of the head and pop 2 brown M&M's on the front of the pink nose to create nostrils.

8 Horns

Time to bring the WOW factor! First up, HORNS! Cut a giant white marshmallow diagonally in half to create 2 triangles. Place the horns on top of the head, keeping them on the inside of the cow's ears.

9 Fluffy Hair

Squeeze the remaining dark-brown buttercream from the piping bag. Don't worry about cleaning the bag. Instead, keep the star tip nozzle in place and fill the bag with the light-brown buttercream. Squeeze until most of the remaining dark-brown buttercream has gone and the light-brown buttercream is coming through. You are now ready to create a fringe! Pipe lines of light-brown buttercream down the face and around the eyes – you can make your cow as hairy as you like. And that's it!

FARM DÖG

it's a challenge!

A farm isn't complete without a farm dog! I love how smart
they are and how much they love their job. From herding
sheep to keeping a farmer company, they truly are the best
companions! My favourite thing about this hack is that, just like
there are many different dogs out in the world, you can follow
the steps and choose any colours to make this dog your own.

You Will Need

25cm round cake board

2 piping bags

1 star tip nozzle

~~~

1 20cm round cake

1 batch Tigga's buttercream (see page 15)

½ batch dark chocolate ganache
(see page 16)

2 tan ice-cream wafers

2 marshmallow eyes (see page 17)

1 chocolate button

Scan for
video tutorial!

Cut the Cake!

Okie dokie, let's get to work!
Cut the cake into 4 pieces as shown.
Start with the longest vertical cut, followed
by the 2 smaller horizontal ones. You
will end up with 4 pieces: the head (1),
muzzle (2) and ears (3 and 4). Carefully trim
down the sides of piece 1 to square off the
head. Feel free to snack on the offcuts!

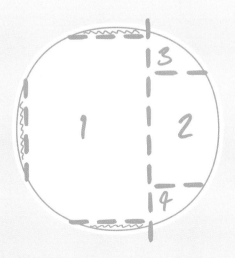

1 Colour

You need 2 colours for this dog. To start, scoop 430g of buttercream into a bowl and leave it white, then colour the remaining buttercream brown by adding spoonfuls of ganache until you have reached the desired colour.

2 Assembly

Spread a little buttercream on the cake board where the cake will sit. This will be the glue that stops the cake from moving around while you are decorating it. Stand the main head piece (1) upright on the board.

Next, stick the muzzle (2) onto the front of your cake using buttercream. Set the ears aside for later.

Shaping

Using a small serrated knife, carefully round off the edges of the muzzle to remove sharp corners.

4 Buttercream Time

Starting with your crumb coat, fill a piping bag with brown buttercream and cut a hole in the end. Roughly pipe over your dog's head, leaving the muzzle bare, and smooth with a palette knife. Empty any remaining buttercream into your bowl and keep the piping bag handy for later use.

Next up, use a separate piping bag filled with white buttercream to pipe over the muzzle and smooth with your palette knife. Chill the cake in the fridge for 10 minutes or until firm. Repeat this process with a second coat for the muzzle only.

5 Blaze

Now it's time to add the blaze to your dog's face – make sure your cake is well chilled before this step. Using your piping bag filled with white buttercream, pipe thick lines in the middle of the dog's head. Carefully smooth out using a palette knife, trying not to disturb the brown buttercream underneath.

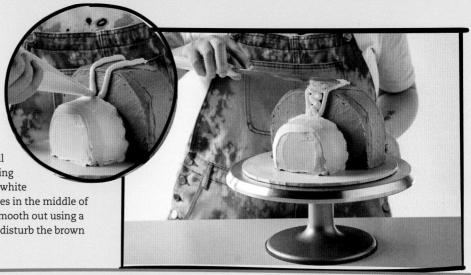

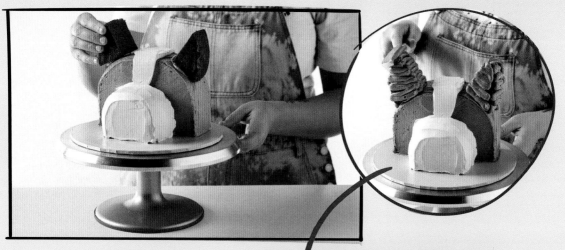

6 Ears

Using buttercream, stick your remaining 2 cake pieces (3 and 4) on top of the head to create the dog's ears. Chill in the fridge for 10 minutes to help them set before moving on. Once the ears feel firm enough, pipe and cover them in the brown buttercream, smoothing out with a palette knife. Finally, cut your wafers into triangles and place them on the front of each ear.

7 Hair

Place your star tip nozzle into your empty dark-brown buttercream piping bag and refill the bag. Pipe buttercream over the entire head (avoiding the blaze) to create your dog's hair.

8 Eyes & Nose

Yay! You're on the home stretch! Now it's time to give your dog some personality! Starting with the marshmallow eyes, place them onto the front of your dog's face. Next up, pop your chocolate button in the centre of the muzzle for the nose.

9 Eyebrows

Lastly, with your white piping bag, pipe some eyebrows above the marshmallow eyes. Using your star tip nozzle for this is optional.

Give yourself a round of A-PAWS!

TRACKS, WHEELS & AUTOMOBILES

All aboard, we're on the move!

Do you remember driving past a construction site when you were a child? It was impossible not to stare, seeing excavators digging into the earth, taking in the noise and sheer size of it all!

There was nothing more exciting!

As we grow older, cars, trucks and trains simply become ways to get us from A to B. We lose the sense of wonder and curiosity. We begin to take for granted the incredible engineering and innovation behind it all.

That's the best part of being a kid. Watching the wheels turn and asking all those same questions . . . 'Where are they going? And how do they work?'

So we're bringing the magic back. From the Monster Truck to the Train Tunnel, these hacks will put you on the track to success!

TRAIN TUNNEL

All aboard the cake hack train! This train tunnel is so effective –
the shape is quite simple and once you add toy trains,
the scene really comes to life. You don't have to do a
crumb coat with this hack, as the whole cake is covered
in edible decorations and none of the buttercream will be
seen! It's the perfect hack to CHOO-CHOO-choose!

*medium!

You Will Need

35cm round cake board

baking paper

1 piping bag

1 20cm round cake (see pages 10–13)

1 133g packet Oreo biscuits

150g white chocolate

1 batch Tigga's buttercream (see page 15)

1 batch edible moss (see page 18)

green gel food colouring

black gel food colouring

2 114g packet Cadbury Fingers

2 toy trains and carriages (optional)

Cut the Cake!

Okie dokie, this cake can be a bit tricky at
the start. Begin by cutting the cake in half
down the centre, then go straight to Step
1 at the top of the next page to guide you.

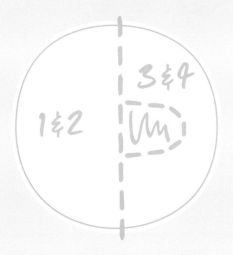

Scan for
video tutorial!

1 Create the Tunnel Shape

Once you have cut the cake down the centre, stand the 2 halves up and slice them down the middle to create 4 semicircles. Two of these will become the tunnel.

Then, using a small, sharp knife, cut a hole on the bottom edge of one of the semicircles – use a glass as a guide, if you like. Make sure the hole is big enough for your toy train, as you will position the train in the tunnel later! Use the offcut piece of cake as a stencil for the second semicircle. This will ensure the tunnel is the same size on both sides. Feel free to snack on the offcut pieces! YUM!

2 Make the Choc Rocks

Have a sheet of baking paper ready. Crush the entire packet of Oreos in a plastic bag with a rolling pin. Scoop out 30g of crushed biscuits, leaving the rest for later. Melt the white chocolate in a microwave-safe bowl in 30-second bursts. Mix the crushed biscuits into the melted chocolate to create a textured grey mixture. Spread a 1cm-deep layer of this mixture onto the baking paper. Chill in the fridge until set.

TRACKS, WHEELS & AUTOMOBILES

3 Colour

Time to colour the buttercream – remember to add the food colouring a little at a time until you are happy with the result. Scoop 430g of buttercream into a bowl and colour it green. Colour the remaining buttercream light grey by adding a little black gel colouring.

4 Stand Upright

Spread some buttercream on the cake board where the cake will sit – this will be the glue that stops the cake from moving around while you are decorating it. Sandwich the uncut semicircles of cake together with green buttercream and stand the cake upright on the board. Attach the tunnel pieces to either side of the cake with green buttercream.

5 Buttercream Time

Cover the outside of the cake with a generous amount of grey buttercream, smoothing it out with a palette knife. Make sure to keep at least 55g of grey buttercream aside for later use. Use the green buttercream to coat the entire board.

6 Train Track

To make the train track, arrange the chocolate finger 'sleepers' over the top of the cake and continue them down onto the board, spacing them evenly. Create more of the train track by placing the chocolate finger sleepers in front of both tunnel openings.

Next, sprinkle the reserved crushed biscuits between the sleepers, filling in the gaps and making sure the sleepers remain visible.

7 Add the Choc Rocks

Roughly chop the set choc rock mixture into pieces with a knife. Use these rocks to surround the tunnel on the front and back of the cake. Any remaining rocks can be used to border the train tracks on the cake board.

8 Moss

Now it's time to use the edible moss you prepared earlier! Break it up into pieces and place it over the top and around the base of the cake, and border the tracks with it.

9 Tracks

Fill a piping bag with the leftover grey buttercream and cut a small hole in the end. Carefully pipe 2 lines of buttercream over the top of the chocolate finger 'sleepers' to create the train tracks.

10 Trains

Time to add your trains! Pick your favourite side and position a train on the tracks, emerging from the tunnel. Place the carriages on the other side to create the illusion that the train is going through the tunnel! Place another train on the top tracks going over the tunnel. TOOT TOOT! Hope you enjoyed the journey!!

ICE-CREAM TRUCK

medium!

On a hot summer's day, is there anything more delightful than hearing the ice-cream truck music? Followed by the shouts of excited children echoing down the street! Just hearing the jingle makes me think of summer and a delicious ice-cream in a cone! With this hack, now you can create your own!

You Will Need

30cm round cake board

1 piping bag

~

1 square 20cm cake (see pages 10–13)

1 batch Tigga's buttercream (see page 15)

pink gel food colouring

teal gel food colouring

4 white round biscuits

1 50g packet Smarties

7 square 100s & 1000s biscuits

3 rectangular ice-cream wafers

1 ice-cream cone

Cut the Cake!

Okie dokie, get excited because this is one of my absolute favourites! Following the cutting guide, cut the cake directly in half down the middle. Piece 1 is the base of the truck. For the second cut, slice down diagonally to create the windscreen on piece 2, which will be the cabin. The remaining bit – piece 3 – will be used to make the ice-cream cone.

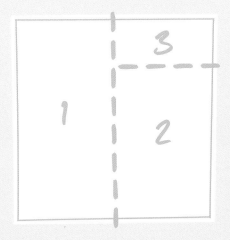

1 Colour

First make the coloured buttercream – remember to add the food colouring a little at a time until you are happy with the result. Scoop 70g of buttercream into a bowl and colour it pink. Colour the rest of the buttercream teal.

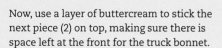

2 Assembly

Spread a little buttercream on the cake board where the cake will sit. This will be the glue that stops the cake from moving around while you are decorating it. Secure the larger cake piece (1) on the cake board.

Now, use a layer of buttercream to stick the next piece (2) on top, making sure there is space left at the front for the truck bonnet.

3 Buttercream Time

Cover the entire cake with teal buttercream, smoothing out using a palette knife and scraper. This is the crumb coat. Chill in the fridge for 10 minutes or until firm. Add a second coat of buttercream, using a palette knife and cake scraper to create a smooth finish. Chill once more in the fridge until firm.

4 Elevate Truck

To give the illusion the truck is sitting off the ground, mark a line along the side of the cake about 1cm up from the cake board. Using a sharp knife, carve diagonally from here into the base of the cake on all sides.

5 Wheels

Attach the 4 round white biscuits onto the sides of the cake to make the wheels. Using buttercream, pop a purple Smartie in the centre of each wheel.

6 Lights & Windows

Use 2 yellow Smarties on the front for headlights and 2 pink Smarties on the rear for brake lights. For the windows, place 2 square 100s & 1000s biscuits on both sides of the truck.

Now, for the windscreen, place 2 more square 100s & 1000s biscuits side by side on the front of your cabin. Lastly, add your remaining biscuit on the back of your truck as the rear windscreen.

7 Bumpers

Cut an ice-cream wafer in half lengthways and fix each one to the cake to form the front and rear bumpers.

TRACKS, WHEELS & AUTOMOBILES

8 Awning

To create the open awning, use a wafer and stick it into the cake so it extends out over the serving window. Cut another ice-cream wafer in half lengthways and secure one half underneath the front window as a ledge. Use the other half as an awning over the windscreen.

9 Ice-cream

Now it's time to make the scoop of 'ice-cream' that will sit on the top of the cake. Smoosh the remaining piece of cake (3) into a ball and place on the roof of the truck. Heat the pink buttercream in a microwave-safe bowl in 10-second bursts until it reaches a pouring consistency. The melted buttercream should be runny, but NOT hot. If it is too hot, it will melt the buttercream icing, so allow it to cool before pouring it on!

Next, mix the melted buttercream well and very gently spoon it over the ball of cake to create a melting 'ice-cream'. The buttercream should cover the ball and pool on the top of the truck. If it drips down the cake a bit, that's okay! Add the ice-cream cone, making sure it's on an angle with the point facing the rear of the truck. And there you have it!

You scream, I scream, we all SCREAM for ICE-CREAM!

MONSTER TRUCK MADNESS

*it's a challenge!

How cool are monster trucks?! These high-octane, adrenaline-pumping machines have MASSIVE wheels that allow them to go just about anywhere. For the wheels on this truck, we have used doughnuts! YUM!

You Will Need

30cm round cake board

2 piping bags

~~~

1 20cm square cake (see pages 10–13)

1 batch Tigga's buttercream (see page 15)

blue gel food colouring

green gel food colouring

4 chocolate doughnuts

2 45g Kit Kats

1 114g packet Cadbury Fingers or similar

yellow M&M's

4 Rolo Milk Chocolates or similar

1 133g packet Oreo biscuits

Cut the Cake!

Okie dokie, following the cutting guide, start with the vertical centre cut and slice your cake into the parts as shown.

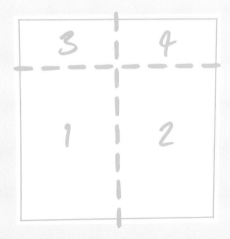

1 Colour

First make the coloured buttercream – remember to add the food colouring a little at a time until you are happy with the result. Scoop 55g of buttercream into a bowl and colour it blue. Colour the rest of the buttercream bright green.

2 Assembly

Now we need to build this monster truck cake nice and high! Secure piece 1 to the cake board with a little buttercream, then put piece 2 on top, securing it with more buttercream.

Next, using a layer of buttercream, stick pieces 3 and 4 together and secure these on top of the cake, making sure there is space left at the front for the truck's bonnet.

3 Buttercream Time

Using a piping bag filled with green buttercream, cover the cake entirely, smoothing out using a palette knife. This is the crumb coat. Chill in the fridge for 10 minutes or until firm.

Then, add a second coat of buttercream. Use a palette knife and cake scraper to achieve as smooth a result as possible.

4 Pop on the Wheels

To create your wheels, place the 4 chocolate doughnuts on the sides of the cake.

5 Wheel Guards

Using your piping bag filled with green buttercream, pipe over the top of the doughnut wheels to form wheel guards, smoothing out with a palette knife. Chill the cake in the fridge for at least 10 minutes or until firm.

6 Windows

Ensure the cake is fully chilled and has hardened before this step. Fill a piping bag with blue buttercream, cut the end off and pipe out a windscreen onto the front of the truck's cabin.

Next, pipe out the blue buttercream onto the side of the cabin to create the windows. Lightly smooth out the windscreen and windows with a palette knife, being careful not to disturb the green buttercream underneath.

7 Accessorise

Using chocolate fingers and Kit Kat, outline the roof and windows of the monster truck. Cut the chocolate fingers in half, place them in a row and pop a Kit Kat finger on top and below to create a front grill. Use yellow M&M's for headlights and rear lights.

Now, pop a yellow M&M in the centre of each doughnut wheel. If the doughnut holes are too big, fill them in with some buttercream. Time to add some roof lights! Using buttercream, stick yellow M&M's onto round chocolates. Attach them to the truck in a row onto the Kit Kat above the windscreen.

8 Dirt

It's not a monster truck without some DIRT! To make the edible dirt, crush the Oreo biscuits using a food processor or a rolling pin. Place the 'dirt' around the base of the truck. AWESOME JOB!

MONSTER effort!

TIGGA'S DIGGER

it's a challenge!

This hack is one of the more tricky cakes in this book, but who doesn't love a good challenge?! Construction and excavation are such popular themes for kids' birthday cakes, and our Tigga's Digger is sure to impress!

You Will Need

35cm round cake board

2 piping bags

~~~

1 20cm square chocolate mud cake (see pages 10–11)

1 batch Tigga's buttercream (see page 15)

blue gel food colouring

yellow gel food colouring

4 large round chocolate biscuits

5 smaller round chocolate biscuits

1 114g packet Cadbury Fingers or similar

1 125g packet Mini Cadbury Fingers or similar

2 marshmallow eyes (see page 17)

1 49g packet M&M's

1 41g packet Rolo Milk Chocolates or similar

1 45g Kit Kat

Cut the Cake!

Okie dokie, let's DIG in! Following the cutting guide, cut the cake into the parts as shown, starting with the vertical cut and following with the smaller cuts.

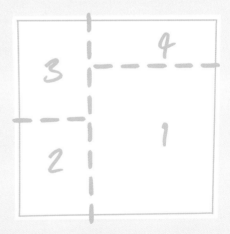

Scan for video tutorial!

1 Colour

First make the coloured buttercream – remember to add the food colouring a little at a time until you are happy with the result. Scoop 55g of buttercream into a bowl and colour it blue. Colour the remaining buttercream bright yellow.

2 Assembly

Set aside piece 4, the digger's bucket. Using a little buttercream as glue, place the largest piece (1) on the cake board. Ensure the cake is positioned slightly towards the back of the board, allowing room at the front for the digger's bucket.

Next, stack pieces 2 and 3 on top of piece 1, securing each layer with some buttercream. Chill the cake in the fridge for at least 10 minutes or until firm.

TRACKS, WHEELS & AUTOMOBILES

3 Shaping

Now that the cake has chilled and the buttercream has hardened, it's time to shape the digger's cabin. In a downward motion, slice the front and back off the cake at an angle. Feel free to eat these offcuts!

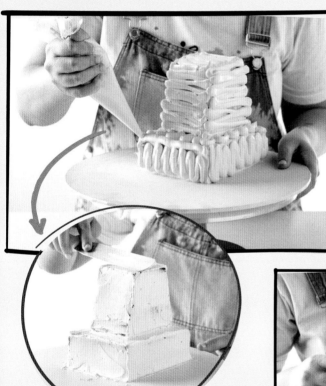

4 Buttercream Time

Fill a piping bag with yellow buttercream and cut off the end. Pipe roughly to cover the entire cake, smoothing out using a palette knife and scraper. This is your crumb coat. Chill in the fridge for 10 minutes or until firm.

Then, add a second coat of buttercream, using a palette knife and scraper to achieve as smooth a result as possible. Chill the cake once more in the fridge for 10 minutes or until firm.

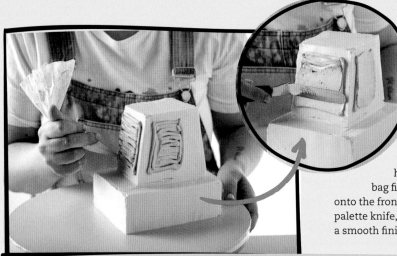

5 Windows

Now it's time for the windows and the windscreen. Ensure the buttercream is fully chilled and has hardened before this step. Using a piping bag filled with blue buttercream, pipe squares onto the front and sides of the digger's cabin. Using a palette knife, smear the blue buttercream to achieve a smooth finish.

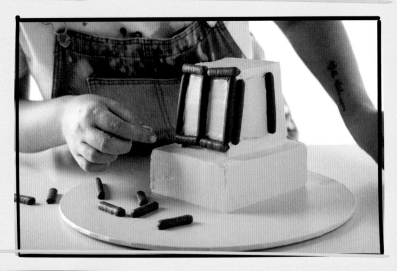

6 Framing

Use the chocolate fingers and mini fingers to frame the windscreen and side windows.

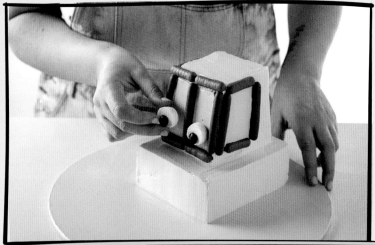

7 Eyes

Pop the marshmallows eyes on the front of the digger's windscreen.

8 Wheels

Next up, we are going to make the wheels – we are doubling up on biscuits to help make the wheels stand out!

To make a rear wheel, stick 2 large chocolate biscuits together using buttercream, then repeat to make the second wheel. Attach the wheels using buttercream. Cut the last of the smaller chocolate biscuits in half, then place one half on the front of the digger to create a mouth. You can eat the other half!

9 Guards

Fill a piping bag with yellow buttercream and cut a hole in the end. Pipe over the top of the biscuit wheels to create the wheel guards. Smooth over with a palette knife.

10 Bumpers

Next, pipe across the front and rear of the cake base to create the bumpers.

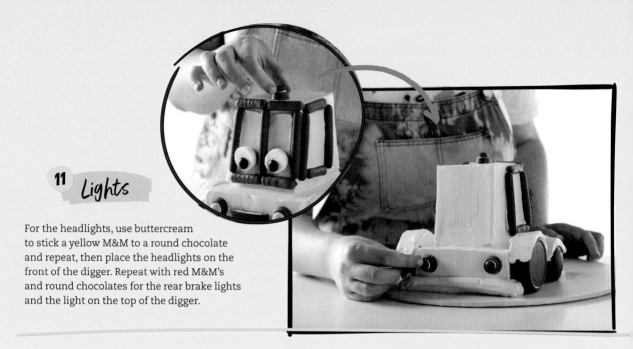

11 Lights

For the headlights, use buttercream to stick a yellow M&M to a round chocolate and repeat, then place the headlights on the front of the digger. Repeat with red M&M's and round chocolates for the rear brake lights and the light on the top of the digger.

12 Starting the Bucket

To make the bucket, carve the remaining piece of cake (4) to create a wedge. Keep the offcuts for later use.

Next, use a Kit Kat finger to measure where to place the bucket in front of the digger – measure out from the corner of the windscreen and position the bucket at the end of the Kit Kat. Secure the bucket to the board with some buttercream.

13 Finishing the Bucket

Cover the entire bucket with yellow buttercream and carefully smooth out with a palette knife. Attach the Kit Kat fingers on either side of the bucket to create the digger's arms, extending from the cake to the sides of the bucket. Use round chocolates as 'bolts', attaching them with buttercream.

14 Cake Dirt

Now it's time to fill your digger's bucket with dirt! Start by breaking the cake offcuts into crumbs. Cover the front of the bucket with the cake 'dirt', making it look like it's full to the brim! Finally, outline the bucket by piping around the edges in yellow buttercream. ALL done! You worked hard and now you get to eat cake! You DIGGIN' it?

SLIMY SCALES, TEETH & TAILS

Adventure calls! Within this chapter you will find yourself trekking through the tallest jungles and wading into slimy swamps.

These hacks are all about connecting with nature. Exploring a sense of danger and thrill that only exists in the wild. Hearing the mighty lions roar or the snap of a hippo's massive jaw. Watching the speed of a snake and the grace of a monkey's swing.

We have created a bunch of wild hacks for you to tame into edible masterpieces. There is something here for everyone!

These hacks vary from the simple Slithery Snake to the more advanced Dino-might!

But rest assured any one of these cake characters will be the perfect centrepiece for a wild party!!

SLITHERY SNAKE

easy peasy!

In just a few sssimple ssssteps you will have a sssuper ssspecial ssslithery sssnake!!! This is one of our quickest, easiest hacks and can even be doubled or tripled in length for larger parties. Get the kids involved in the decorating – they can add the finishing colourful touches to create the scaly pattern!

You Will Need

35cm round cake board

1 piping bag

8cm round cutter

~~~

1 20cm round cake (see pages 10–13)

1 batch Tigga's buttercream (see page 15)

orange gel food colouring

1 180g packet M&M's or Smarties, sorted in colours

2 marshmallow eyes (see page 17)

1 red jelly snake

Cut the Cake!

Okie dokie, let'ssss get ssssstarted! Following the cutting guide, push the round cutter into the centre of the cake (2), then cut the rest of the cake as shown.

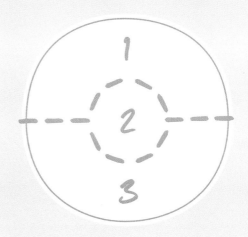

1 Colour

First make the coloured buttercream – remember to add the food colouring a little at a time until you are happy with the result. Colour the buttercream orange.

2 Assembly

To make the snake's slithery body, lay your pieces onto the cake board before attaching them with buttercream, to ensure they are in the right position. Place piece 1 onto the cake board using a little buttercream as the glue. Keep this piece on the right-hand side of the board in the shape of a rainbow. Attach the round head (2) to the board on the far right end. Lastly, attach the remaining piece (3) to the other end.

3 Shaping

To round off the snake's body, use a sharp knife to carve the edges away from the cake. Keep these offcuts as you will use them to help build up the snake's tail. To help achieve a pointy tail, start by carving off the sides at the end of the snake. Now squish all of the offcuts into a point and attach this to the end of the snake with a little buttercream. To give the snake a more realistic head, carve the edges into a more triangular shape. Squish those offcuts onto the front of the head to finish the look, securing with buttercream if needed.

SLIMY SCALES, TEETH & TAILS

4 Buttercream Time

Fill a piping bag with the orange buttercream and cut off the end. Roughly cover the entire head and body with buttercream and smooth out using a palette knife. This is your crumb coat. Chill in the fridge for 10 minutes or until firm. Add a second coat of buttercream, using a palette knife to achieve as smooth a result as possible.

5 Pattern

Arrange the M&M's down the snake's body in any pattern you would like! As you can see, I went with stripes!

6 Eyes & Tongue

Pop the marshmallow eyes onto the head. For the snake's tongue, cut the red jelly snake in half. Using scissors, snip a 'V' in the end to create a forked tongue and attach it to the head. Snap some pics and ssssmile at your masterpiece!

HIP-HIP HAPPY HIPPO

Fun fact about hippos: they can't swim! They trot along the bottom of the riverbed and can hold their breath for up to 5 minutes. Can you see our happy hippo peeping out of the water waiting for the party to start?

You Will Need

30cm round cake board

2 piping bags

1 party hat (optional)

1 20cm round cake (see pages 10–13)

1 batch Tigga's buttercream (see page 15)

blue gel food colouring

black gel food colouring

2 pink marshmallows

2 marshmallow eyes (see page 17)

2 brown M&M's

Cut the Cake!

Okie dokie, time to get started! Following the cutting guide, cut the cake slightly off centre followed by the two smaller cuts on either side.

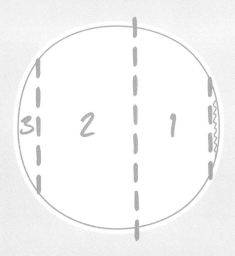

1 Colour

First make the coloured buttercream – remember to add the food colouring a little at a time until you are happy with the result. Scoop 215g of buttercream into a bowl and colour it blue. Colour the remaining buttercream grey by adding a drop of black to the white buttercream.

2 Assembly

Spread a little buttercream on the cake board where the cake will sit. This will be the glue that stops the cake from moving around while you are decorating it. Stand the hippo's head piece (1) upright on the board. Place the hippo's nose piece (2) up against the head but lying down flat on the board.

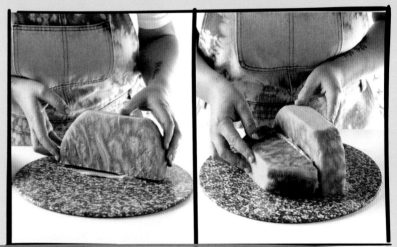

3 Shaping

It's time to give the hippo some shape! Cut piece 3 in half and secure the pieces on top of the nose with buttercream.

SLIMY SCALES, TEETH & TAILS

4 Buttercream Time

Fill a piping bag with grey buttercream and cut off the end. Roughly cover the entire head, smoothing out using a palette knife. This is the crumb coat. Chill in the fridge for 10 minutes or until firm. Add a second coat of buttercream, using a palette knife to achieve as smooth a result as possible.

5 Ears

To create the ears, press 2 pink marshmallows onto the top of the hippo's head.

Now, pipe over the top and back of the ears in grey buttercream. Then chill in the fridge for 15 minutes or until firm.

6 Eyes & Nostrils

Add the marshmallow eyes to the hippo's face and 2 brown M&M's to the nose for nostrils.

7 Water

Fill a piping bag with the blue buttercream and cut off the end. Pipe the buttercream around the hippo.

Finally, use a palette knife to spread the buttercream over the board and to create ripples in the water. There you have it! Add a colourful party hat and it's officially a Hip-Hip Happy HIPPO!

MERRY MONKEY

medium!

Monkeys are cheeky and mischievous! Let's face it, we can all take life a little too seriously sometimes, and this hack is the perfect reminder to have some fun in the kitchen!

You Will Need

20cm round cake board

2 piping bags

baking paper

2 toothpicks (optional)

~~~~~~~

1 20cm round cake (see pages 10–13)

1 batch Tigga's buttercream (see page 15)

brown gel food colouring or 1 batch dark chocolate ganache (see page 16)

2 brown M&M's

2 pink marshmallows

2 marshmallow eyes (see page 17)

1 white marshmallow

Scan for video tutorial!

Cut the Cake!

Okie dokie, stop monkeying around and let's do it! Following the cutting guide, cut the cake as shown, starting with the long vertical cut. The offcuts won't be needed and are the perfect snack to keep you going. Enjoy!

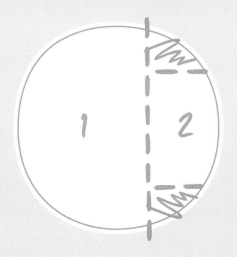

1 Colour

You need 2 different colours for the monkey. To start, scoop 430g of buttercream into a bowl and colour it light brown using food colouring or a small amount of ganache. Then colour the remaining buttercream dark brown by adding spoonfuls of ganache until you have reached the desired colour.

2 Assembly

Spread a little buttercream on the cake board where the cake will sit. This will be the glue that stops the cake from moving around while you are decorating it. Stand the head piece (1) upright on the board.

3 Buttercream Time

Fill a piping bag with the dark-brown buttercream and cut off the end. Roughly cover the entire head with buttercream, smoothing out using a palette knife. This is the crumb coat. Chill in the fridge for 10 minutes or until firm. Add a second coat of buttercream, using a palette knife to achieve as smooth a result as possible. Pop the cake back in the fridge until firm before moving on. Keep any remaining dark-brown buttercream and the piping bag for the ears later on.

4 Monkey's Face

Fill a piping bag with the light-brown buttercream and cut off the end. Pipe the shape of the monkey's face onto the chilled cake. Smooth out using a palette knife or cake scraper.

5 Attaching & Shaping

Attach piece 2, the nose, on the front of the monkey's face. Using a small knife, carve the corners off the nose to round it off.

6 Buttercream Nose

Pipe on the light-brown buttercream to cover
the monkey's nose completely. Smooth out using
a palette knife.

7 Eyes & Nose

Place the marshmallow eyes on the front of the monkey's
face. Add the M&M's to make the nostrils. Good job!
The face is now complete.

8 Ears

To create the ears, pipe 2 blobs of dark-brown buttercream onto a piece of baking paper. Press a pink marshmallow into each blob and flatten gently, then chill in the fridge for 15 minutes or until firm.

Once firm, slice the bottoms off each blob to create a flat edge and using buttercream, stick the ears onto the monkey's head. If you are worried about the ears falling off, we would recommend using toothpicks to secure them in place! Just remember to remove the toothpicks before serving!

9 Finishing Touches

For extra cuteness, let's add some hair! Using the remaining dark-brown buttercream, pipe some 'hair' between the ears. Give your monkey a cheeky smile by adding a slice of marshmallow on the front of the cake. Go BANANAS! You've just created a very merry monkey.

ROARSOME LION

medium!

Enter the jungle and get ready to meet the king! Our ROARsome lion is the perfect addition to any WILD party. My favourite part of this hack is the biscuit mane as it really brings this lion to life.

You Will Need

25cm cake board

2 piping bags

baking paper

2 toothpicks (optional)

~~~

1 20cm round cake (see pages 10–13)

1 batch Tigga's buttercream (see page 15)

yellow gel food colouring

brown gel food colouring

3 pink marshmallows

2 marshmallow eyes (see page 17)

8 round chocolate biscuits

Cut the Cake!

Okie dokie, let's begin! Following the cutting guide, cut the cake as shown starting with the long vertical cut. You will end up with 2 main pieces – the head (1) and the muzzle (2) – plus 2 small offcuts. Feel free to snack on these offcuts, as you won't need them!

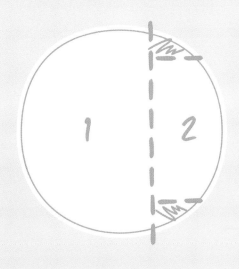

Tigga's Tips ★

Take off the biscuit mane and change the colour of the buttercream to turn this lion into a BEAR!

1 Colour

First make the coloured buttercream – remember to add the food colouring a little at a time until you are happy with the result. Colour all the buttercream pale yellow and add a drop of brown to turn it pale gold. Scoop 215g of pale-gold buttercream into a bowl and set it aside. This will be for the lion's muzzle. Continue adding more yellow and brown to the remaining buttercream until you achieve a rich dark-gold colour. This will be for the lion's head.

2 Assembly

Now it's time to put the pieces together. Spread a little buttercream on the cake board where the cake will sit. This will be the glue that stops the cake from moving around while you are decorating it. Stand the head (1) upright on the board.

Then, use buttercream to stick the muzzle (2) to the front of the head. Remember, a nice cold cake is much easier to handle!

SLIMY SCALES, TEETH & TAILS

3 Carving

The lion's head is now coming together. To complete the shape, use a small, sharp knife to round off the edges of the muzzle. Also cut a small triangle from the top of the muzzle to allow room for the nose.

4 Buttercream Time

Fill a piping bag with the dark-gold buttercream and cut off the end. Roughly pipe buttercream all over the head (but NOT the muzzle), smoothing out with a palette knife. Fill the other piping bag with the light-gold buttercream and pipe over the muzzle, once again smoothing out with a palette knife. Chill the cake for at least 10 minutes or until firm. Add a second coat of each buttercream colour, using a palette knife to achieve as smooth a result as possible.

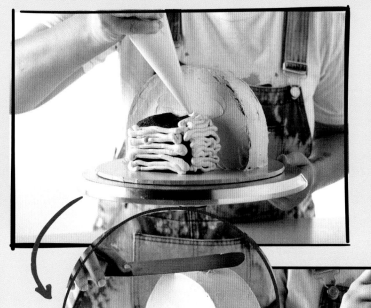

Now, mark a line down the centre of the muzzle using a wooden skewer. Set the remaining dark-gold buttercream aside to add details later on.

5 Nose & Eyes

For the nose, cut a pink marshmallow into a heart shape using scissors and pop it into place. Place the marshmallow eyes on the front of the head.

6 Ears

To create the ears, pipe 2 blobs of dark-gold buttercream onto a piece of baking paper. Press a pink marshmallow into each blob and flatten gently, then chill in the fridge for 15 minutes or until firm.

Once firm, slice the bottoms off each blob to create a flat edge and using buttercream, stick the ears onto the lion's head. If you are worried about the ears falling off, you can add toothpicks to secure them in place! Just remember to remove the toothpicks before serving!

The Mane Event

Cut the bottom third off each chocolate biscuit to create a flat edge.

Then pipe a line of dark-gold buttercream around the head to secure the biscuits and place them side by side to form the mane.

Finally, using the remaining dark-gold buttercream, pipe some hair on top of the lion's head. Now that your cake is complete, step back and admire your creation with PRIDE!

ROARsome job!

FANCY FROG

medium!

Grab your tiaras and top hats and roll out the red carpet –
Fancy Frog is here! Watch as this fun and fancy frog hippity
hops its way into your fantastical party dreams.

You Will Need

25cm round cake board
2 piping bags
baking paper
2 toothpicks (optional)
1 ribbon (optional)

~~~~~

1 20cm round cake (see page 10–13)
1 batch Tigga's buttercream (see page 15)
yellow gel food colouring
green gel food colouring
2 marshmallow eyes (see page 17)
1 white marshmallow

Cut the Cake!

Okie dokie, let's jump to it! Following
the cutting guide, start with the long
vertical cut followed by the smaller cuts.

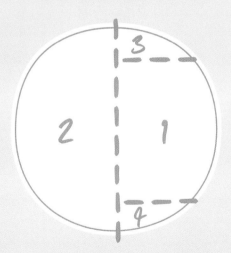

Tigga's Tips ★

If you are concerned the
eyes might fall off, we recommend
putting toothpicks in the eyes
to secure them in place – just
remember to remove them
before serving!

1 Colour

First make the coloured buttercream – remember to add the food colouring a little at a time until you are happy with the result. Scoop 55g of buttercream into a bowl and colour this lime green, this can be achieved by adding a drop of yellow into pale green. Colour the remaining buttercream green.

2 Assembly

Spread a little buttercream on the cake board where the cake will sit. This will be the glue that stops the cake from moving around while you are decorating it. Place piece 1 towards the front of the cake board and sandwich piece 2 behind it with buttercream.

Then, use buttercream to stick pieces 3 and 4 on top of piece 1. This will help to build up the shape of the frog's head.

SLIMY SCALES, TEETH & TAILS

3 Buttercream Time

Fill a piping bag with green buttercream and cut a hole in the end. Roughly cover the entire frog with buttercream, smoothing out using a palette knife. This is your crumb coat. Place in the fridge for 10 minutes or until firm.

When ready, add a second coat of buttercream, using a palette knife to achieve as smooth a result as possible. Keep any remaining green buttercream and your piping bag for later use.

4 Belly

Ensure the buttercream is fully chilled and has hardened before this next step. To create the frog's belly, fill a second piping bag with lime green buttercream and pipe a semicircle onto the bottom half of the front of the cake. Carefully smooth out using a palette knife, trying not to disturb the green buttercream underneath.

5 Eyes

To make the eyes, use your original piping bag with green buttercream. Pipe 2 blobs of buttercream onto a piece of baking paper. Flatten them slightly with a palette knife. Place a marshmallow eye onto the centre of each green buttercream blob, so you have two froggy eyes. Put them in the fridge for 10 minutes or until firm.

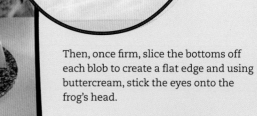

Then, once firm, slice the bottoms off each blob to create a flat edge and using buttercream, stick the eyes onto the frog's head.

6 Legs & Mouth

Using the same piping bag, pipe the front legs onto the frog's belly with green buttercream and add the feet to the board in front of each leg. Pipe the back feet onto the board on either side of the cake. For the mouth cut a piece of marshmallow and place it on the front of the cake. Then, if you are feeling fancy, use a ribbon to create a bow tie and place it on the frog using a bit of buttercream to attach it.

This calls for cake!
XOXO
OKIE DOKIE
KISS ME
XOXO
LOVE
HUGS
MILK

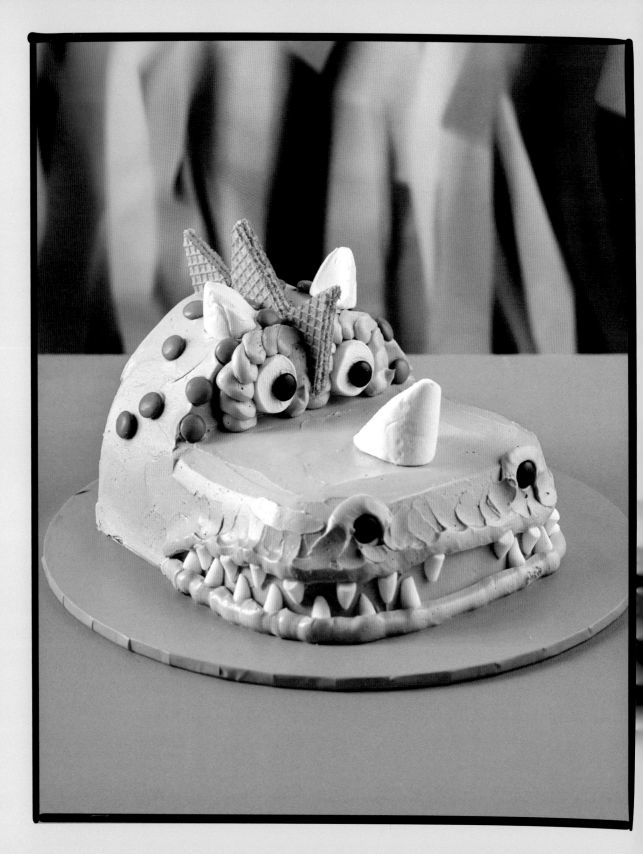

DINO-MIGHT

Scaly, spotty and spiky, this mighty dinosaur will suit any dino-themed party. But watch out! The rows of 'sharp' marshmallow teeth are sure to leave you running in terror!

You Will Need

30cm round cake board

1 piping bag

~~~

1 20cm round cake (see pages 10–13)

1 batch Tigga's buttercream (see page 15)

blue gel food colouring

2 marshmallow eyes (see page 17)

1 white marshmallow

1 giant white marshmallow

1 180g packet M&M's
(we only use the orange and brown ones)

1 100g packet mini white marshmallows

3 pink wafers

Cut the Cake!

Okie dokie! Ready, set . . . DINO! Following the cutting guide, cut the cake into parts as shown. You will end up with 1 and 2 as the main, larger pieces and 3, 4 and 5 as the smaller pieces. The tiny offcuts can be eaten!

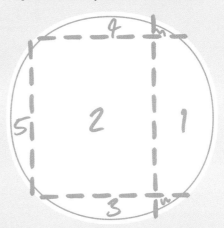

Scan for video tutorial!

1 Colour

First make the coloured buttercream – remember to add the food colouring a little at a time until you are happy with the result. Colour all the buttercream bright blue.

Tigga's Tips ★

Colour your cake green and take the spikes off and BAM! You've got yourself a crocodile cake!

2 Assembly

Spread a little buttercream on the cake board where the cake will sit. This will be the glue that stops the cake from moving around while you are decorating it. Stand the head piece (1) upright towards the back of the board.

Then carefully place the dinosaur's snout (2) firmly up against the head, lying down flat.

SLIMY SCALES, TEETH & TAILS

3 Shaping

This next step is to give some height and shape to the dinosaur's head. Using buttercream, stick pieces 3 and 4 side by side on the dinosaur's head. Cut the remaining piece (5) in half.

Now, use a little buttercream to attach both pieces to the top of the dino's head, leaving a small gap between them. Then, use a small knife to cut the edges around the snout – you now have the completed shape of your dino.

4 Buttercream Time

It's time to give your dinosaur some COLOUR! Fill a piping bag with blue buttercream and cut a hole in the end. Roughly pipe over the entire cake, then smooth out the buttercream with a palette knife. This is the crumb coat. Chill in the fridge for 10 minutes or until firm. Add a second coat of buttercream, using a palette knife to achieve as smooth a result as possible.

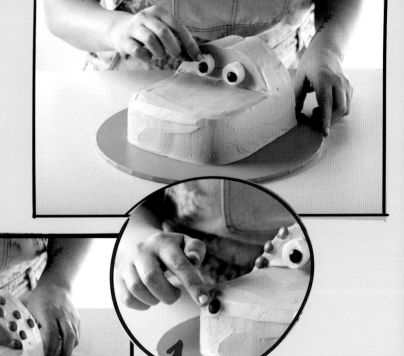

5 Eyes & Nose

Now it's time to bring your dino to life! Pop the marshmallow eyes onto the front of the dino's head.

Then, arrange orange M&M's around the eyes and over the head to create a scaly effect. For the nostrils, place 2 brown M&M's on the front of the nose.

6 Dinosaur Smile

Okay, get excited – this next bit is my absolute favourite part! To make the dinosaur's sharp teeth, use a pair of scissors to cut the mini marshmallows in half diagonally. Arrange them in 2 rows across the front and sides of the dino's mouth.

SLIMY SCALES, TEETH & TAILS

7 Piping

Pipe a line of blue buttercream along the top and bottom rows of teeth. Using a small palette knife, blend the top line of buttercream in small strokes.

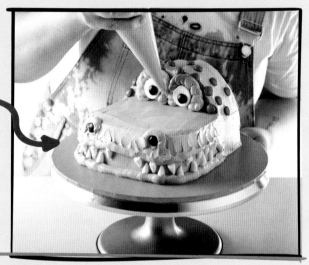

Now, add some piping over the top of the nostrils and around the eyes. Look! Your dino is almost complete!

8 Spikes & Horns

The dinosaur's spikes really bring this hack home. Cut a giant white marshmallow in half diagonally to create a horn on the front of the dino's snout. Cut the regular marshmallow in half diagonally and place the 2 smaller horns on top of the dino head. Cut the wafers into triangles and poke the triangle spikes on top of the dinosaur's head extending down the neck. There you have it, dino spikes — *YIKES!*

CREEPY, KOOKY

&

ALL THINGS SPOOKY

BOO! Did I scare you??

Get ready to creep out your party guests with these delicious creations! Why choose between trick OR treat when you can do both! This chapter is the ultimate combination of creepy and cute!

The spider is groovy, the ghost is kinda friendly, the monster is full of surprises and the bloody brain . . . well the brain is actually quite gross and not for the faint-hearted!

Halloween is finally starting to take off here in Australia, and I'm all for it! No matter what age you are, getting dressed up in costumes, sharing and eating sweets – what's not to love!

BLOODY BRAIN

*easy peasy!

Follow the blood trail and be prepared to be GROSSED OUT!
The perfect trick or treat at any spooky celebration!
I love how simple this hack is but as soon as you add
the jam BLOOD it's enough to creep anyone out.

You Will Need

25cm round cake board

1 piping bag

1 large round piping tip

1 sieve

~~~

1 20cm round cake (see pages 10–13)

1 batch Tigga's buttercream (see page 15)

red gel food colouring

1 375g jar raspberry jam

Cut the Cake!

Okie dokie, following the cutting guide,
cut the cake in half down the middle.

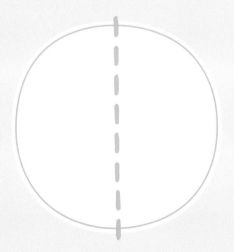

1 Colour

First make the coloured buttercream – remember to add the food colouring a little at a time until you are happy with the result. Colour the buttercream pale pink.

2 Assembly

Spread a little buttercream on the cake board where the cake will sit. This will be the glue that stops the cake from moving around while you are decorating it. Sandwich the 2 cake halves together with a layer of buttercream and stand the cake upright on the board.

3 Buttercream Time

Using a palette knife, cover the entire cake in pink buttercream. This is the crumb coat. It doesn't have to be perfect as you will be piping over it! Chill in the fridge for 10 minutes or until firm.

CREEPY, KOOKY & ALL THINGS SPOOKY

4 BRAAAIIIINNNNS

Pop the round piping tip into your piping bag and fill the bag with pale pink buttercream. Using a palette knife or skewer, mark out a line down the centre of your cake, to create the two hemispheres of the brain. Pipe squiggly lines on either side until the entire brain is covered. Chill the cake in the fridge for 30 minutes or until completely firm. It is important to make sure the cake is fully chilled before moving on to the next step.

Tigga's Tips ★
Make extra pink buttercream and use the same piping technique for matching brain cupcakes!

5 Blood

For the blood, we are going to use jam. Place it in a bowl and stir in a little warm water. If your jam is not red enough, add some red gel colouring to the jam to make it look more like BLOOD. Strain the jam through a sieve to remove any seeds and lumps. Using a pastry brush, carefully apply the jam all over the brain until it is covered and add some splatters to the cake board to create a terrifying blood-soaked scene!

GHASTLY GHOST

*easy peasy!

Do you believe in ghosts? Even if you're a non-believer, things are about to get a little spooky! Our friendly little ghost will be loved by girls, guys and GHOULS of all ages. Let this sweet spirit haunt your next party!

You Will Need

25cm round cake board
1 piping bag
1 round piping nozzle

2 15cm round cakes (see pages 10–13)
1 batch Tigga's buttercream (see page 15)
purple gel food colouring
icing sugar
3 Oreo or similar chocolate biscuits

Cut the Cake!

Okie dokie, slice each cake in half horizontally to create 4 even layers.

This one gets sliced to make layers!

1 Stacking

Spread a little buttercream on the cake board where the cake will sit. This will be the glue that stops the cake from moving around while you are decorating it. Stack the 4 layers on top of each other on the board, layering with approximately 105g of buttercream in each layer as you go. Chill the cake in the fridge for at least 10 minutes or until firm.

2 Carving

To make a ghostly shape, you need to round off the top of the cake. Using a sharp serrated knife, carefully carve the edges of the cake away in a downward motion to create a dome shape. These trimmings are yours to enjoy!

3 Buttercream Time

Add a single drop of purple gel colouring to the buttercream to help neutralise the yellow and make it appear whiter. Roughly pipe over the entire cake, smoothing out using a palette knife. This is the crumb coat. Chill in the fridge for 10 minutes or until firm. Add a second coat of buttercream, this time making short strokes with the palette knife to create a textured finish.

CREEPY, KOOKY & ALL THINGS SPOOKY

4 Arms

This next step will work best with firm buttercream. If you find your buttercream is too soft, pop it in the fridge for 5 minutes to firm it up. Give it a stir before placing it in the piping bag with a round piping nozzle. You will note in the picture that the ghost's arms are thicker at the base and thinner at the top. To create this look, pipe in an upwards motion using more pressure at the base and reducing the pressure as you move upwards. Once the arms are in place, chill the cake in the fridge for at least 10 minutes or until firm.

5 Eyes & Mouth

Now it's time to make your ghost scream! Split apart your 3 Oreo cookies and use the cookie halves with no icing. Feel free to eat the icing halves! Using scissors, shape your Oreos into oval shapes.

6 Finishing Touches

Carefully put the Oreo eyes and mouth onto the cake, gently pushing them into place. This will help give the illusion of black holes in your ghost's face.

Creepy! BOO-tiful job!

DANCING SPIDER

Yes, it's true, spiders can be TERRIFYING! From their furry little bodies to their creepy crawly legs, it's easy to see why people run scared. But our spider is the exception! Cute, fluffy and ready to boogie, you're sure to fall in love, just like we have!

* medium!

You Will Need

25cm round cake board

1 piping bag

1 grass tip nozzle

8 black or brown pipe cleaners

~

1 20cm round cake (see pages 10–13)

1 batch Tigga's buttercream (see page 15)

brown gel food colouring

2 marshmallow eyes (see page 17)

Cut the Cake!

Okie dokie, following the cutting guide, start with the long vertical cut and cut the cake as shown. You will have 2 main pieces and 2 small offcuts. You won't need the offcuts, so feel free to snack on them as you go!

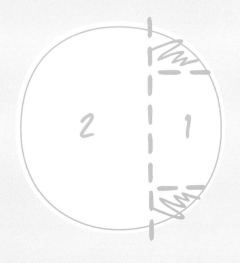

Tigga's Tips ★

As an alternative to gel colouring, you can also make the chocolate buttercream for the spider by adding ganache (see page 15).

1 Colour

Time to make the coloured buttercream – remember to add the food colouring a little at a time until you are happy with the result. Add brown gel colouring to the buttercream to colour it dark brown.

2 Assembly

Now it's time to put the pieces together. Spread a little buttercream on the cake board where the cake will sit. This will be the glue that stops the cake from moving around while you are decorating it. Stand the larger body piece (1) upright on the board.

Then, use buttercream to stick the head piece (2) to the front of the spider's body. Chill the cake in the fridge for 10 minutes or until firm and secure.

CREEPY, KOOKY & ALL THINGS SPOOKY

3 Carving

Next up, let's shape the spider's head! Using a small, sharp knife, round off the edges of the head by carving the corners away.

4 Buttercream Time

Fill a piping bag with the brown buttercream and cut off the end. Roughly pipe over the entire cake and smooth out using a palette knife. This is the crumb coat. Chill in the fridge for 10 minutes or until the buttercream is firm.

Next, add a second coat of buttercream to the head ONLY, using a palette knife to achieve as smooth a result as possible. You don't need to do a top coat on the body as it will be piped over.

5 Hairy Piping

Pop the grass tip nozzle into the piping bag and fill the bag with more buttercream. Pipe over the entire spider's body (NOT the head) to create a 'hairy' look! Leave the spider's head smooth.

6 Eyes

Pop the marshmallow eyes onto the head. I've used 2 but you can use as many eyes as you'd like! Some spiders have 8 eyes!

7 Legs

Bend the pipe cleaners into shape before poking them into each side of the body. Your spider is complete! Give the board a wiggle and watch your spider dance!

CREEPY, KOOKY & ALL THINGS SPOOKY

MONSTER MAYHEM

*medium!

This one-eyed monster is full of surprises! It may be cute and furry on the outside, but don't be fooled – this monster will cause mess and mayhem!

You Will Need

25cm round cake board

6cm round cutter

2 piping bags

1 grass tip nozzle

cling film

~~~

2 15cm round cakes (see pages 10–13)

1 batch Tigga's buttercream (see page 15)

190g assorted sweets

purple gel food colouring

blue gel food colouring

2 giant white marshmallows

green M&M's

1 chocolate button

Cut the Cake!

Okie dokie, let's get going! Start by cutting both cakes in half horizontally, creating 4 layers. Separate the layers out on your bench. Using the cutter, cut a hole in the centre of 3 layers. Leave the last layer whole.

Scan for video tutorial!

1 Stacking

Fill a piping bag with white buttercream, then cut a hole in the end. Stack the 3 layers with the holes on top of each other with a layer of piped buttercream between each one. Fill the hole with the assorted sweets. Using buttercream, stick the final layer on top as a lid. Chill the cake in the fridge for 10 minutes or until firm.

2 Carving

To make a monster shape, you need to round off the top of the cake. Using a sharp serrated knife, carefully carve the top edges of the cake away in a downward motion until you have achieved a rounded shape. Feel free to eat the offcuts!

3 Buttercream Time

Using a palette knife, cover the entire cake in buttercream. This is the crumb coat. It doesn't have to be perfect as you will be piping over it! Chill in the fridge for 10 minutes or until firm.

CREEPY, KOOKY & ALL THINGS SPOOKY

4 Colour

Now we are going to give the monster some multicoloured hair! This step is a bit time consuming, but the end result is worth it. First make the coloured buttercream – remember to add the food colouring a little at a time until you are happy with the result. Divide the remaining buttercream between 2 bowls. Colour one bright purple and the other bright blue. Set aside 70g of purple buttercream for later use.

5 Piping Bag

Prepare the piping bag by popping in a grass tip nozzle. Set aside. Next up, place a 40cm piece of cling film on your bench. This type of piping works best with firm buttercream. If you find your buttercream is too soft, pop it in the fridge for 5 minutes to firm up, then give it a stir. Spoon the purple and blue buttercream onto the cling film, side by side. Roll up the cling film to create a buttercream 'sausage' and twist the ends, then cut off the excess cling film at one end. Put the buttercream, cut-end down, into the prepared piping bag.

6 Hair

Pipe mad monster hair over the entire cake! You may need to refill your bag – if so just pull out the cling film and refill the same bag with a new cling film 'sausage' of buttercream.

Then, when the cake is fully covered, pull out the cling film and clean the piping bag, and keep it aside for later use.

7 Horns & Hair

To create the monster's horns, cut a giant white marshmallow in half diagonally. Place the horns on top of the monster's head. Place a grass tip nozzle into your piping bag and using the reserved purple buttercream, pipe out a tuft of fringe in between the horns.

You could even add more marshmallow eyes for an extra-kooky look!

8 Eye & Teeth

Next up, cut a giant white marshmallow in half to make 2 round pieces. One will become the monster's eye, the other will be used for the monster's teeth. For the eye, place a chocolate button on the sticky side. Place the eye on the front of the cake.

Now, for the teeth, cut the other half of the giant white marshmallow into triangles. Place them into 2 rows to create a smile.

9 Finishing Touches

Finally, use the green M&M's to create a spotty monster. Now all that's left to do is to cut into your masterpiece and reveal the surprise inside!

TRUE AUSSIE DELIGHTS

Okie dokie and g'day mate! This chapter is a real ripsnorter!
As most of you would know, I'm a true AUSSIE (or fair dinkum Aussie,
as we say over here)!

From days at the beach to nights spent camping
in the bush, I couldn't resist sharing some beaut
examples of classic Aussie culture!

The 'Okie dokie' catchphrase in my strong Aussie accent
has always been a fun way to connect online and the perfect
convo starter with people across the globe. There is nothing
quite like the skill of an Aussie to abbreviate everything!
We have a knack for throwing an 'o' or an 'ee' sound onto the
end of every word, and to me it just sounds like home.

The Aussie laid-back attitude of 'No worries!' and
'She'll be right!' is the perfect way to approach creating
these hacks. Because at the end of the day, it's just a cake!

So, gear up and give these hacks a crack!

FAIRY BREAD CAKE

easy peasy!

Fairy bread is an absolute Aussie classic at every kid's party but (confession time!), I hate fairy bread! The combination of bread, butter and 100s & 1000s has just never been a winner to my tastebuds. So, instead I came up with an alternative that uses vanilla cake instead of bread, and buttercream instead of butter. It looks just like traditional fairy bread but it's EVEN BETTER. Have fun tricking your party guests!

You Will Need

1 serving board or platter

1 20cm square vanilla cake
(see pages 12–13)

½ batch Tigga's buttercream
(see page 15)

yellow gel food colouring

1 190g packet 100s & 1000s

Cut the Cake!

Okie dokie, following the cutting guide, cut the cake diagonally to create 4 triangles.

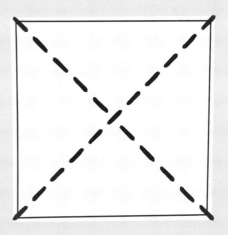

1 Slice the Bread

Stand each triangle upright and slice downwards to produce 8 even triangles.

If you want smaller slices and more serves, simply cut each triangle in half and you'll end up with 16 slices.

2 Colour

Now it's time to make the 'butter'. Colour the buttercream pale yellow. Remember to add the food colouring a little at a time until you are happy with the result. Try to get your colour as buttery as possible!

Don't be afraid to lay it on thick!

3 Buttercream Time

Making sure you don't go all the way to the edges, spread a layer of buttercream on each triangle.

Tigga's Tips ★
Don't like 100s & 1000s? No rules here – use any sprinkle you like!

4 Time to Sprinkle

It's not fairy bread without the 100s & 1000s! Sprinkle them over the buttercream, shaking off any excess. Arrange the fairy bread on a board or platter and Bob's your uncle. You've got fairy bread, except it's cake!

SANDCASTLE CAKE

medium!

No beach day is complete without a sandcastle. That feeling of lifting the bucket and seeing your castle suddenly appear is magical. Now you can bring this sandcastle to life – and take a bite!

You Will Need

baking paper

25cm round cake board

1 rolling pin or food processor

1 silicone shell mould

1 piping bag

1 pastry brush

1 small flag (optional)

15g puffed rice cereal

10g butter

6 white marshmallows

225g white chocolate

2 15cm round cakes

1 batch Tigga's buttercream
(see page 15)

yellow gel food colouring

1 250g packet Rich Tea biscuits
or similar

5 ice-cream cup cones

Cut the Cake!

Okie dokie, no need to cut this yet – it will be done later in Step 7!

We'll cut some layers later!

Scan for video tutorial!

1 Crush & Melt

Let's get BEACHY! First step is to make a batch of delicious puffed rice marshmallow slice. Roughly crush the puffed rice with a rolling pin. Melt the butter in a microwave-safe bowl, then set aside. Melt the marshmallows in another microwave-safe bowl for 30 seconds. Combine the crushed puffed rice, melted butter and marshmallows and mix thoroughly.

2 Press & Shape

Tip the marshmallow mixture into a mound on a large piece of baking paper. Fold the baking paper over the mound and press and shape the mixture into a square about 2cm high. Place in the fridge to set.

3 Chocolate Shells

Place the chocolate in a microwave-safe bowl. Microwave in short bursts, stirring in between until completely melted. Fill the silicone mould. Let the chocolate set in the fridge.

TRUE AUSSIE DELIGHTS

4 Crush It

Time to create your edible 'sand'! Crush the biscuits in a food processor or in a plastic bag with a rolling pin until you have fine sandy crumbs. Transfer the crumbs to a large, wide bowl.

5 Colour

Colour all the buttercream a sandy yellow with the yellow gel colouring. Remember to add the food colouring a little at a time until you are happy with the result.

6 Ice-cream cones

Using a serrated knife, cut off the side of 4 of the ice-cream cones, leaving the last cone whole. Using a pastry brush, lightly brush buttercream over the cones and roll them in the crushed biscuit 'sand'. Set aside.

7 Stacking

Start by cutting both cakes in half horizontally, creating 4 layers. Spread a little buttercream on the cake board where the cake will sit. This will be the glue that stops the cake from moving around while you are decorating it. Stack all 4 layers on top of each other with a generous layer of buttercream between each one. Chill the cake in the fridge for 10 minutes or until firm.

8 Buttercream Time

First up, let's do a crumb coat. Cover the entire cake in buttercream and smooth out using a palette knife and cake scraper. Chill in the fridge for 10 minutes until firm.

9 Carving

Create a door by making a hole in the front of the cake using a spoon. Cover the cake in a second coat of buttercream, smoothing out with a palette knife and scraper – try your best to achieve a nice sharp edge!

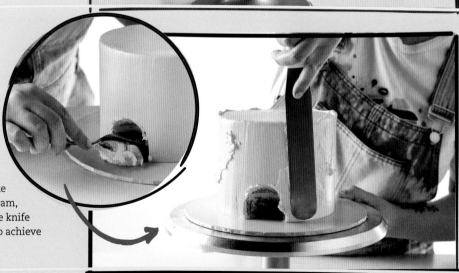

TRUE AUSSIE DELIGHTS

Now it's time to cover the cake in edible sand. This may get a little messy, but that's okay! Cover the sides of the cake using your hands. Leave the top of your cake sand-free for now but keep the extra 'sand' aside for later.

11 *Cones*

Next step is attaching the ice-cream cones you prepared earlier. First, stick the uncut cone to the top of the cake. Then fill a piping bag with the remaining yellow buttercream and pipe around the cut edges of the other cones.

Now attach those 4 cones around the cake, making sure they are evenly spread and touching the cake board.

12 Turrets

Take the puffed rice marshmallow slice out of the fridge. Using a sharp knife, cut it evenly into 8 squares.

Now, tip these squares into the bowl of leftover 'sand' and toss them until evenly coated. Using the piping bag, pipe a little buttercream onto each sandy square, then place them evenly around the border of the cake.

Level up the look by dusting your shells with edible shimmer dust!

13 Finishing Touches

Pop the chocolate shells out of their mould and, using buttercream, attach them around the front of the cake. If you have a flag, attach it to the top of the castle. Pipe some buttercream around the base of your cake and sprinkle the remaining 'sand' over the top of the cake and around the base. TA DA! You're the queen or king of the castle!

LET'S GO CAMPING

it's a challenge!

It's time to set up camp! This hack is perfect for any camping enthusiast. Follow these steps and you will have everything you need to set the scene: loads of dirt, chocolate rocks, edible moss and a perfectly pitched tent. You will even have your own campfire!

You Will Need

35cm round cake board
baking paper
1 rolling pin
1 piping bag
birthday candles

~~~

1 square cake (see pages 10–13)
1 133g packet Oreo biscuits
150g white chocolate
1 batch Tigga's buttercream (see page 15)
1 batch edible moss (see page 18)
green gel food colouring
orange gel food colouring
2 ice-cream wafers

Scan for video tutorial!

Cut the Cake!

Okie dokie, following the cutting guide, cut the cake diagonally to create 4 triangles. Three of these pieces will make the tent. Keep the fourth piece for the campfire.

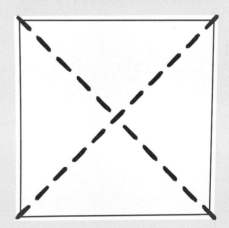

Tigga Mac's **CAKE HACKS**

1   Make the Choc Rocks

In a plastic bag, with a rolling pin, crush the entire packet of Oreos. Scoop out 30g of crushed biscuits, leaving the rest for later. Have a sheet of baking paper ready. Melt the white chocolate in a microwave-safe bowl in 30-second bursts. Mix the 30g of crushed biscuits into the melted chocolate to create a textured grey mixture. Spread a 1cm-deep layer of this mixture onto the baking paper. Chill in the fridge until set. Once set, roughly chop the chocolate into pieces with a knife to create chocolate 'rocks'.

2   Colour

Time to make the coloured buttercream – you will be making 2 colours. Remember to add the food colouring a little at a time until you are happy with the result. Colour 215g green. Colour the remaining buttercream orange.

3 Assembly

Spread a little orange buttercream towards the back of the cake board where the cake will sit, allowing room for the campfire in front. Stick the 3 triangles onto the cake board, sandwiching together with buttercream.

4 Buttercream Time

Cover the tent with a crumb coat of orange buttercream, smoothing it with a palette knife and a cake scraper to achieve sharp lines. Chill the cake in the fridge for 10 minutes or until firm.

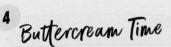

Then, repeat the process with a final coat of buttercream, once again smoothing out with a palette knife and scraper.

5 Tent Flaps

While you are waiting for your tent to firm up in the fridge, let's make the tent opening! Cut a rectangular wafer in half diagonally to produce 2 triangles. Flip one of the triangles over and cover them in orange buttercream. Chill them in the fridge on a piece of baking paper.

6 Campfire

Coat the entire board with green buttercream. To make the campfire you need to use some of the remaining cake triangle. Break the cake into pieces and smoosh just enough of it together to create a mound of 'dirt' on the buttercream-covered board in front of the tent.

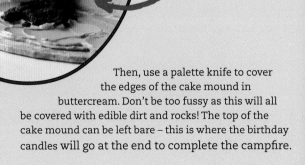

Then, use a palette knife to cover the edges of the cake mound in buttercream. Don't be too fussy as this will all be covered with edible dirt and rocks! The top of the cake mound can be left bare – this is where the birthday candles will go at the end to complete the campfire.

7 *Dirt*

Place the remaining crushed biscuits all over the buttercream-covered board to create 'dirt'.

8 *Rocks*

Now it's time for the choc rocks! Place them in a circle around the campfire and scatter any leftover rocks around the tent.

9 *Moss*

Break up the edible moss and place it around the camp site!

10 Tent Flaps & Windows

Attach the wafer tent flaps to the front of the cake, leaving a triangular opening. Cut the other wafer in half to create 2 squares and place these on both sides of the tent to create windows.

11 Finishing Touches

Now it's time to take your tent to the next level! Fill a piping bag with orange buttercream and cut a small hole in the end. Pipe across the top of the cake, down each side of the tent, around the windows and then the edges of the tent flaps. Pipe some semicircles along the base of the tent on both sides. This will give the illusion of tent pegs. Pipe a line of buttercream down the middle of the back of the tent.

Lastly, pipe a thick line of buttercream along the top of each window to create rolled-up window covers. When it's time to sing 'Happy Birthday', simply cut the candles to make them a bit shorter, poke them into the campfire cake mound, light the campfire and make a wish!

CUDDLY KOALA

it's a challenge!

When it comes to Aussie animals, they don't get much cuter than the cuddly koala. Unlike most of our other cakes where we cut them before adding the buttercream, this hack uses a 'cake-top forward' technique. This means you will be covering the cake with buttercream before slicing a small portion off one side and then standing it up so the top faces forward.

You Will Need

25cm round cake board

baking paper

2 piping bags

1 star tip nozzle

1 20cm round cake (see pages 10–13)

1 batch Tigga's buttercream (see page 15)

black gel food colouring

3 round chocolate biscuits (we use McVitie's Digestives as they cut easily)

2 marshmallow eyes (see page 17)

1 pink marshmallow

Cut the Cake!

Okie dokie, this happens at Step 3, so wait until then before cutting the cake as shown.

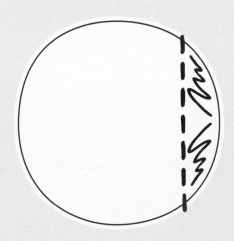

1 Colour

Set aside 215g of buttercream for later. Colour the rest of the buttercream grey by adding some black gel colouring – remember to add the food colouring a little at a time until you are happy with the result.

2 Buttercream Time

Spread a little buttercream on the cake board to secure your cake temporarily. This will be the glue that stops the cake from moving around while you apply the crumb coat and are decorating it. Cover the cake in a light crumb coat of grey buttercream using a palette knife and smoothing it with a cake scraper. Don't be too fussy as you will be covering the whole cake in piping! Chill the cake in the fridge for at least 15 minutes or until firm.

3 Cutting

Following the cutting guide, slice the side off the cake. You don't need this offcut, so feel free to eat it!

4 Stand It Up

Have a sheet of baking paper ready alongside the cake board. Slide a palette knife underneath the cake and transfer the cake from the board to the baking paper. Clean the cake board before moving on.

Next, spread a little buttercream on the cake board where the cake will sit. Stand the cake on the board cut-side down and with the top forward. Pop the cake back into the fridge to firm up.

5 More Buttercream

You'll notice the back of your cake is naked! Using a palette knife, coat the back of the cake in a crumb coat of grey buttercream and smooth with a palette knife and cake scraper. Chill in the fridge for 10 minutes or until firm.

6 Fluff

Now it's time to make your koala fluffy!
Fit a piping bag with a star tip nozzle
and fill it with grey buttercream. Cover
the entire cake in piping. This may be
a time-consuming process but the end
result is worth it!

7 Ears & Chin

Using a small knife, make a cut in each
side of the head where the koala's ears
will go. Firmly stick a biscuit into each
cut. Leaving the front of the ears bare,
pipe grey buttercream over the top and
backs of the ears. Remove the nozzle
and give it a wash.

Next, fit the nozzle to the second piping
bag and fill it with the reserved white
buttercream. Pipe over the front of the
ears and create a chin by piping a small
semicircle in the middle, at the base
of the cake. Keep the bag aside to add
some furry eyebrows in a later step.

TRUE AUSSIE DELIGHTS

8 Nose

Carve the remaining biscuit with a small, sharp knife into an oval shape, and pop it in place for the nose.

9 Eyes & Cheeks

Place marshmallow eyes on the front of the cake. Use a pink marshmallow cut in half for rosy cheeks. Lastly, pipe eyebrows above the eyes! After all that hard yakka, you've got yourself a cuddly koala. Give yourself a pat on the back.

Glossary

100s & 1000s

100s & 1000s are a type of sprinkle. They are tiny balls of multicoloured sugar that can be sprinkled over cakes and desserts.

Baking paper

Also known as parchment paper, this is a type of paper with a special non-stick surface that is also heat resistant. Note: Greaseproof paper is not the same as baking paper!

Cake board

A flat support under a cake that makes it easy to lift and transport. Cake boards come in a variety of colours, shapes and sizes.

Cake knife

A serrated knife with a long blade that is used to cut and slice through cakes.

Cake scraper

This decorating tool with a firm blade is made from stainless steel, acrylic or plastic. It may or may not come with a handle for a more comfortable grip. It is used to smooth out your buttercream.

Cake stacking

The process of cutting your cake into even layers and placing them on top of each other, layering with buttercream.

Crumb coat

The first coat of buttercream that catches all the crumbs from your cake. This first layer is then chilled until firm before the second (and final) coat of buttercream goes on.

Edible glitter and shimmer

A decorative ingredient used to give sparkle or shimmer to your cakes. It is suitable and safe for use in all edible elements on your cake.

Food processor

An appliance with blades used for shredding, blending or chopping food.

Gel food colouring

A water-based concentrated form of food colouring.

Oil-based food colouring

An oil-based concentrated form of food colouring.

Palette knife

A flat, wide knife with a rounded edge. It is used in cake decorating for spreading, smoothing and applying buttercream.

Piping bag

A triangular-shaped bag used to fill with icing to decorate your cake. It may be used with or without a piping tip.

Piping tip

This is a nozzle that attaches to the end of a piping bag. There are many different piping tips out there. The ones used for the cake hacks in this book are star tip nozzle, grass tip nozzle and round nozzle.

Rolling pin

A rolling pin is a cyclindrical utensil used to shape or flatten dough. It can also be used to crush biscuits.

Rubber spatula

A flat utensil used for mixing, spreading and scraping.

Sprinkles

Sprinkles are small pieces of coloured sugar or chocolate used as a decoration.

Stand mixer

A heavy-duty electric mixer attached to a stand that sits on a countertop.

Turntable

This is an elevated stand for your cake to sit on that can rotate smoothly.

Index

Conversion Charts

(Measures are approximate, rounded to nearest whole number)

Length measures

metric	imperial
10cm	4in
15cm	6in
20cm	8in

Dry measures

metric	imperial
60g	2oz
90g	3oz
120g	4oz
150g	5oz
180g	6oz
200g	7oz
225g	8oz
250g	9oz
300g	10oz
340g	12oz
375g	13oz
500g	18oz
620g	22oz

Liquid measures

metric	imperial
60ml	2 fluid oz
180ml	6 fluid oz
200ml	7 fluid oz
250ml	8 fluid oz
300ml	10 fluid oz

Oven temperatures

180°C	350°F

Hack Difficulty Index

QR Codes Menu

Tigga's **CHOCOLATE MUD CAKE**
pages 10–11

TIGGA'S DIGGER
pages 112–119

Tigga's **VANILLA VELVET CAKE**
pages 12–13

MERRY MONKEY
pages 132–137

Tigga's **BUTTERCREAM**
page 15

DINO-MIGHT
pages 150–155

YOU ARE MY SUNSHINE
pages 36–41

MONSTER MAYHEM
pages 172–177

MAGICAL MERMAID TAIL
pages 50–53

SANDCASTLE CAKE
pages 184–190

FARM DOG
pages 86–91

LET'S GO CAMPING
pages 192–198

TRAIN TUNNEL
pages 94–99

My Cake Creations

This is a space for you to keep a record of all of your cake masterpieces! That way the memories will live on long after the final crumbs are gone!

Acknowledgements

Writing this book has been more challenging and rewarding than I ever could have thought possible, and it wouldn't have happened without all the love and support of our favourite humans.

To my beautiful Nana Betty. You are the most wonderful person I know. Thank you for showing me that whatever life throws our way, we can get through it. Your resilience and determination are so inspiring. I love you to bits!

To my little shrub, thank you for your support and encouragement along the way. Having a little sister like you is rare, you are one of my best friends and biggest supporters. I love ya!

To my papa bear. Dad, I wish you were here to see this. You would have given me a cuddle with tears in your eyes, never afraid to show me how proud you are. I miss you.

To my second dad! D, far out you're amazing. Thank you for being with us every step of the way and for putting your hand up whenever we needed help. Can't even begin to express how much I love and appreciate you.

Mum. What can I say? I am who I am because of you. Growing up, you always made us kids believe that we could do anything! Nothing was out of reach for us. 'Dream big!' you would say. Well, we dreamed and we made that dream come true! But it wouldn't have happened without you. Thank you so much, Mumsy. I love you to the moon and back.

To my main man. Eam, you are my constant. Sixteen years together and we have never wavered. When I set out with my besty to build my very own cake biz, you didn't baulk. You said, 'DO IT!' You picked up the slack financially and gave me the push and support I needed. You believed in me and cheered me on like my very own bearded cheerleader. So thank you. I love you SUPER MASSIVE.

Finally, to Katie, my BESTY BAKER BIZ PARTNER! Holy moly, what a wild ride these last few years have been. I know without a doubt that I wouldn't have been able to do any of this without you. You believed in me and made this happen. You opened your house up to the crazy cake life and it has been the best years of my life. Going in to work every day with my best friend is an absolute dream come true. You are more than my besty. You are my family.

We joke that you're the accelerator and I'm the brakes. But it couldn't be more true. You push me and encourage me every day and I want to thank you for being the driving force that made our small biz happen. I'm so glad that all those years ago, you approached the new girl crying on a bench at school and said hello.

To my family and friends, thank you so much for your ongoing support. For always encouraging my creativity and showing such enthusiasm for every milestone the Tigga Mac brand achieves.

To my parents, Ann and Phil. There is no way I would have been able to co-write this book without you. You have provided me with unwavering support my entire life.

After raising four children of your own, you continue to help me to raise my four beautiful children and give me the time and freedom to pursue my own career.

Mum, you inspired my love of baking from such a young age. Thanks for always letting me help in the kitchen and for filling our home with the sweetest memories. Your love and support means the world to me. Thank you.

Dad, you never hesitate to drop everything to help everyone around you. By starting your own business you inspired me to start mine. When it seemed hopeless, you were the one who suggested converting our spare room into a kitchen. None of this would have happened if you hadn't lit the spark. Thank you.

To my husband Marc: I adore this crazy, chaotic, beautiful family we have created together.

Thank you for always letting me be completely myself, which means you don't always get the best of me. You also get the tired me, the overwhelmed me, the stressed and anxious me, the hyperactive me. But you love me regardless. I hope I make you proud. I love you.

To my four beautiful children – Lily, Hannah, Lewis and Maeve. This book has been such a huge achievement but my biggest achievement has been you guys.

So many of my contributions and ideas in this book came from being your mum. Witnessing you all grow and guiding you along the way has been the greatest privilege of my life. You are all my sunshine and my reason for it all. I love you.

Lastly, to Tigga. Wow. I still can't quite believe what we have accomplished together. Becoming your friend over 20 years ago is one of the things in life I will always be most grateful for. I have adored being your business partner and best friend. Seeing your creative genius grow over these years has been something I never tire of or take for granted. You are truly gifted.

But outside of business you are one of the most important people in my life. It's a rare gift to have someone in your life who knows all of you. Who is a part of your most precious memories and moments. And you have been there, through it all. Making me laugh and providing a shoulder to cry on.

I can't wait to continue on this journey with you, to keep climbing and reach new heights. But I also hope we both take a moment to pause, to take in the view and appreciate how far we have come and what we have accomplished. We wrote a book!

I love you. Thank you for this dream job of going to work every day with my best friend.

Katie x

Wow. It's still hard to believe that we wrote a book. An actual proper BOOK!

Two years ago it was a crazy dream.

A year and a half ago we started thinking, *Maybe we actually can . . .*

We had no idea where to start or what was involved but we figured it out and learned a lot along the way.

We've met so many amazingly talented people who believed in our concept and helped bring it to life.

To the team at Penguin Random House, who despite our complete lack of experience in the world of publishing have gently and kindly guided us through the entire journey. Ashwin, Izzy and Adam, we are so grateful for your expertise. You understood our vision from the very beginning and ensured that the book reflected the Tigga Mac vibe in every way!

To Fergus and the High Spot Literary team.

Fergus, we are still so grateful that you responded to our initial vague email and understood our mission! You have taught us so much and really held our hands while we took our first steps into the world of publishing!

To Brent and Meryl, the geniuses behind the photography and food styling for our book. You both welcomed us into the studio with open arms. Thank you for creating such a fun atmosphere, where we felt completely at ease.

Brent, your passion and dedication to the art of photography and food is inspiring!

Meryl, having you on set every day gave us such a sense of reassurance. You have such a good eye and responded so enthusiastically to any idea we sent your way.

To our team at Changer Studios. You boys, in particular Lee, have been instrumental in building the Tigga Mac brand into a legitimate and reputable business.

Lee, your skills, knowledge and loyalty to us and our brand has been amazing. You have advocated for us in every way and made us see our worth and understand our value. We are so grateful to have met you.

To our dear friends Manda, Bree and Meaghan, thank you so much for your help during our photography shoot! It was a massive few weeks for us and having you there to help made everything more fun!

Manda, you are the ultimate cheerleader and the other side of the triangle. You have provided support and unwavering friendship for years and please don't ever doubt how much that means to us. You are an invaluable member of our team. Thank you for being YOU!

To Julia and Doiren, you have both been such a wonderful support throughout the years. Whenever we need you, there is no absolutely no hesitation. You are there. From helping out at the photography shoot, to offering creative advice and support in both our lives. It means the world to both of us.

Lastly, we need to thank our audience. You are the reason we were able to create this book. Every video and photo that was viewed, every like and comment shared.

When we opened up our little kitchen to the world we never expected to build such an incredible community. A community of all ages across the globe who have cheered us on and lifted us up.

Tigga Mac has always been about trying to provide a colour-filled, sweet world of escape for everyone.

We have worked so hard to create this book and it's no longer just ours, it is now a gift that belongs to everyone who wants to give cake decorating a go! For their children and their children's children.

The fact that we have such an incredibly fun, creative and fulfilling job is thanks to you! We pinch ourselves every day so thank you, thank you, thank you.

Tigga & Katie x